ALCATRAZ

ALCATRAZ

HISTORY AND DESIGN OF A LANDMARK

Donald MacDonald and Ira Nadel

CHRONICLE BOOKS

SAN FRANCISCO

Library of Congress Cataloging-in-Publication Data available.

ISBN: 978-1-4521-0153-8

Manufactured in China

Designed by Lynda Lucas

10 9 8 7 6 5 4 3 2 1

Chronicle Books LLC
680 Second Street
San Francisco, California 94107
www.chroniclebooks.com

TABLE OF CONTENTS

INTRODUCTION

Whenever civilized nations occupy an island, they turn it either into a fortress or a prison. —PASCAL

Island prisons begin with Crete, where Icarus escaped from the labyrinth with his son Daedalus by fashioning wings and flying toward the sun. Napoleon imprisoned at Saint Helena, Dreyfus at Devil's Island, and Nelson Mandela at Robben Island are more recent inmates of infamous and isolated prisons. Château d'If, a French island prison a mile or so off Marseille, housed the fictional Count of Monte Cristo, while Mussolini sent political opponents to the Lipari Islands off the Italian coast. In his *Gulag Archipelago*, Alexander Solzhenitsyn described the notorious Solovki island monastery prison, at one time also the "home" of the writer Maxim Gorky. On the East Coast of the United States, Governor's Island, a former U.S. military base in New York harbor, held a prison where Revolutionary and Civil War spies were hanged. And on the West Coast was Alcatraz, the federal prison where there were no executions but where no one ever escaped.

Architecture plays a crucial role in understanding Alcatraz because it encloses the prison's mystery and danger. The well-known but opaque and imposing cellhouse became the dominant image of the island, visible—from a distance—throughout the Bay Area. It stood as the external expression of the prison's internal purpose—punishment, discipline, and control—while maintaining the intrigue and secrecy of the prison by revealing nothing to the public. The harsh microclimate of the island began to undermine the cellhouse's materials and structural integrity, however, and it soon began to deteriorate. And as it began to wear down, so too did the purpose of the prison, which closed in 1963.

And its name, "The Rock"? It originated with the soldiers stationed there during World War II to guard the harbor, the term conveying the isolation and remoteness of the island. No other name would suit the barren land and rocky formations.

Until recently, distance has always defined Alcatraz. From the brick and masonry fortress and Citadel to the concrete and imposing cellblock, one can see its history in its buildings and understand its past. The variety of styles, from the "Third System" of defensive forts to the Victorian and mission revival styles, link the island to the mainland and yet maintain its distinction. The federal style of the massive cellblock (started in 1909) contrasts with the more discrete and individualistic styles of the Officers' Quarters or the New Industries Building, built with an eye on the modern.

The very distance and secrecy of Alcatraz, imposed by nature and reiterated by its architecture, increased attention on the things most visible from the mainland: its buildings. With their enclosed and hidden functions, the structures intensified the curiosity of the public (normally prevented from visiting prisons) as to exactly what went on there. And when the prison was finally opened to the public, the number of visitors was staggering. It was a chance to find out the secrets of the island, which only the buildings, seen from a distance, could suggest—or hide.

This book tells the long history of Alcatraz through its architecture and inhabitants, from its earliest discovery through its use as a military fortress, federal penitentiary, occupied site, and finally national park. It is a story of the constant remaking of the island, physically and architecturally, and how this isolated sandstone rock became one of America's most visited tourist attractions.

CHAPTER 1

WHAT'S IN A NAME?

Alcatrazes, Alcatras,
Alcatrasas, Alcatraces,
Alcatrose, Alcatrazas,
Alcatrzos, Alcatases,
Alcatrasses, Alcatraz

—ISLAND NAMES, NINETEENTH-CENTURY U.S. ARMY REPORTS

It was not until 1542 that a Spanish explorer named Cabrillo became the first European to navigate the coast of present-day California. Throughout the seventeenth century, more Spaniards arrived to explore the coast, and on November 2, 1769, Gaspar de Portola, on an overland journey, discovered San Francisco Bay—by accident. He was looking for Monterey Bay but found something larger. Six years later, the Spanish explorer Juan Manuel de Ayala and his flotilla arrived by sea.

Ayala, piloting the first recorded ship to enter San Francisco Bay on August 5, 1775, named what is today Yerba Buena Island, two miles east of Alcatraz, Alcatraces after its plentiful pelicans. For the next fifty years, Spanish charts identified the modern Yerba Buena as Alcatraces, while Alcatraz Island remained an anonymous, if large, rock in the middle of the bay, the tip of a submerged mountain. (*Figures 1-2*)

The islands remained so named (and unnamed) until 1827, when a British officer, Captain Fredrick Beechey, shifted the names on Ayala's map, giving the designations used today. He moved the name Alcatraces to one of the unnamed rocks inside the Golden Gate, and the island Ayala originally named Isla de los Alcatraces became Yerba Buena ("good herb"). Until 1822, Alcatraz technically remained the property of the king of Spain. When Mexico achieved independence, however, jurisdiction shifted to the new country, although there was little interest in the island until 1846. That year, Julian Workman, a naturalized

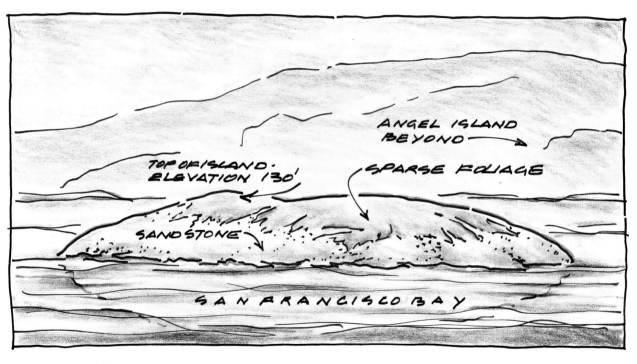

ALCATRAZ ISLAND VIEWED FROM
SAN FRANCISCO'S NOB HILL · 1853

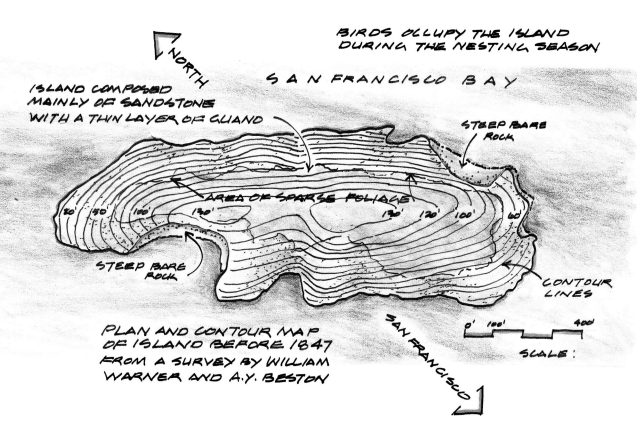

BIRDS OCCUPY THE ISLAND
DURING THE NESTING SEASON

SAN FRANCISCO BAY

ISLAND COMPOSED
MAINLY OF SANDSTONE
WITH A THIN LAYER OF GUANO

STEEP BARE
ROCK

AREA OF SPARSE FOLIAGE

80' 50' 100' 130' 130' 130' 100' 60'

STEEP BARE
ROCK

CONTOUR
LINES

PLAN AND CONTOUR MAP
OF ISLAND BEFORE 1847
FROM A SURVEY BY WILLIAM
WARNER AND A.Y. BESTON

SAN FRANCISCO

0' 100' 400'

SCALE:

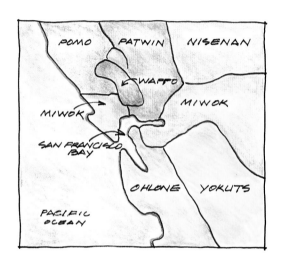

TULE REEDS
BUNDLED

MAP OF SAN FRANCISCO BAY AREA
SHOWING TRIBAL AREAS BEFORE
THE ARRIVAL OF THE SPANISH

TYPICAL SAN FRANCISCO BAY INDIAN BOAT
PRE·1800'S MADE OF TULE REEDS AND USED
FOR 2000 YEARS

FLAG OF THE "BEAR FLAGGERS"
1846
ABOVE IMAGE IS A REPLICA OF THE
ORIGINAL FLAG

Mexican citizen, obtained a land grant; the only condition was that he had to establish a navigation light.

At the conclusion of the Mexican-American war in 1848, the United States refused to recognize all private claims of ownership: The island became public land, secured from Mexico. Alcatraz became the property of the U.S. government. (*Figures 3–5*)

CHAPTER 2

THE DEFENSIVE TRIANGLE: FROM CITADEL TO FORTRESS

The most prominent position of this
secondary line is Alcatraz Island.
Its guns sweep a larger expanse
of waters than those of any other
point . . . —REPORT, PACIFIC BOARD OF ENGINEERS, APRIL 1856

Upon acquiring Alcatraz from Mexico, the U.S. government
acted quickly, immediately recognizing the value of the island.
Anticipating the construction of fortifications, Lieutenant
William Warner and a team of army engineers conducted a survey of Alcatraz Island in 1847. Within a year, gold was discovered in the American River near Placerville, and San Francisco
was caught up in the California gold rush. The world flocked
to San Francisco, and the need for harbor fortifications became
essential. In April 1849, a joint army-navy commission met to
recommend defensive measures for the bay, and on November 1,
1850, they announced their plan, beginning with construction
of two masonry forts at the narrowest part of entry: one at Lime
Point on the northern marine shore and another at Fort Point
on the south bay shore, where a Spanish battery once stood.
The two forts could concentrate cannon fire on any invading
force. But a swift ship might run past the outer batteries, requiring
a third battery of cannons on the island. An island fortress in the
middle of the inner harbor had strategic importance. Its poten-
tial firepower could cover not only the outer batteries to the west,
but also the entire harbor between Angel Island to the north and
San Francisco to the south.

Following President Fillmore's executive order of
November 6, 1850, which reserved certain lands around the
bay for "public purposes," the transformation of the rocky
island into a suitable base for a fortress began almost at once.
For almost fifty years, the army carved and blasted the bluffs of

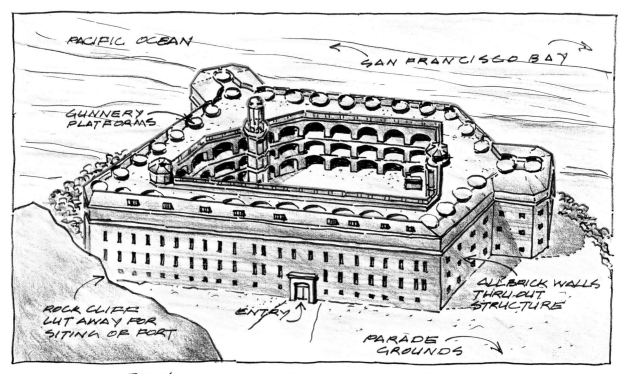

PACIFIC OCEAN

SAN FRANCISCO BAY

GUNNERY
PLATFORMS

ALL BRICK WALLS
THRU-OUT
STRUCTURE

ROCK CLIFF
CUT AWAY FOR
SITING OR PORT

ENTRY

PARADE
GROUNDS

BIRD'S EYE VIEW OF FORT POINT COMPLEX
AS BUILT IN 1861

DASHLINE SHOWING LOCATION OF EXISTING BRIDGE

ROCK CLIFF CUT AWAY FOR SITING OF FORT

ALL BRICK CONSTRUCTION MARIN HILLS BEYOND

VIEW OF FORT POINT AT ENTRY TO SAN-FRANCISCO BAY   AS BUILT IN 1861.

the island to build a ring of gun batteries. The island's high cliffs offered natural protection, and the engineers enhanced this existing escarpment by removing the gentler slopes to create a perpendicular height of twenty-five feet all the way around. But the sandstone that comprised the island was unsuitable for construction and prone to sliding when disturbed. Even when hardened, it could be cut with a hatchet, and a spike could be driven into the rock without much trouble. So, as the natural topography was leveled, foreign soil was introduced: New dirt barged over from Angel Island could cushion any incoming shells and fortify the gun batteries.

Construction of the Alcatraz fortress was daunting. Everything had to be ferried out—not only laborers but also supplies, equipment, food, and even water. The island offered no natural shelter against rain or heat, and dampness persisted, intensified by the almost incessant fog. There was only one possible landing spot, a small cove on the east side. Nonetheless, in the early summer of 1852, engineers began to work out formal plans of construction.

The defensive works were part of the Third System of American fortifications, the third generation of coastal forts built by the United States. They were generally comprised of a single large building with cannons mounted on the roof and projecting from slits in the walls. The traditional casement fort was built from plans similar to those for Fort Sumner in Charleston, South Carolina, where the first battle of the Civil War occurred. Although almost forty forts would eventually be built under the Third System, only Fort Point and Alcatraz would be built west of the Mississippi. (*Figures 6–7*) Construction at Fort Point began in 1853, whereas plans for Lime Point, the third site in the defensive triangle, never materialized, because of difficult negotiations between the U.S. government and the landowner. Despite its original conception as a mere safeguard in the defensive triangle, and the physical and logistical challenges of building its citadel, construction on Alcatraz was completed first.

Behind masonry walls, smoothbore, muzzle-loading Columbiad cannons were placed on the north, south, and west to cover incoming ships. Eventually 111 cannons encircled the island, each gun battery named for prominent Civil War Union officers; temporary guns appeared in 1854. The island was fully garrisoned in 1859, becoming the only permanent U.S. fortification west of the Mississippi. By the end of the Civil War, batteries surrounded the southeastern shore of the island, with gunnery terraces twisting partway around its northeastern end. (*Figures 8–9*)

Ironically, the guns were never fired in either a defensive or an offensive operation. Of the two occasions when they were fired, the first, in 1865, was to mark the funeral of Abraham Lincoln, a symbolic honoring of the sixteenth president. The second was during an exercise to mark the one hundredth anniversary of the United States, on July 3, 1876: In a mock battle, an explosive-laden barge was towed into the bay, and guns from Alcatraz and Fort Point were to display their accuracy by hitting it. Neither succeeded, and the Alcatraz guns were especially off target. Only after a young officer went out and lit the barge on fire did the spectacular display of exploding gunpowder and ammunition occur.

Near the lighthouse was a defensive barracks unofficially named the Citadel. Sturdy brick walls broken by narrow rifle-slit windows formed the first level; the upper story offered living quarters. The basement housed kitchens, dining halls, water, food stores, and other supplies. Soldiers entered the Citadel by crossing a drawbridge that spanned a dry moat. The Citadel could hold a hundred men in peacetime and two hundred if under attack. Supplies allowed for a four-month siege. Built

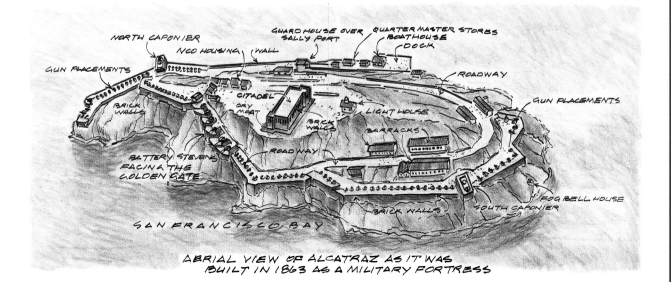

AERIAL VIEW OF ALCATRAZ AS IT WAS
BUILT IN 1863 AS A MILITARY FORTRESS

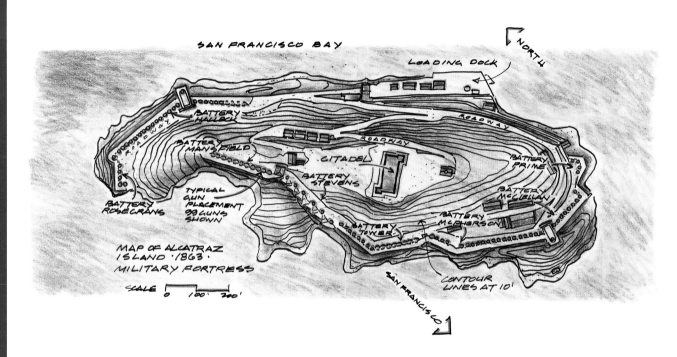

SAN FRANCISCO BAY

LOADING DOCK

NORTH

ROADWAY

BATTERY
HALLECK

ROADWAY

BATTERY
MANSFIELD

CITADEL

BATTERY
PRIME

BATTERY
STEVENS

BATTERY
McCLELLAN

BATTERY
ROSECRANS

TYPICAL
GUN
PLACEMENT
99 GUNS
SHOWN

BATTERY
TOWER

BATTERY
McPHERSON

MAP OF ALCATRAZ
ISLAND ·1863·
MILITARY FORTRESS

SCALE
0   100'   200'

SAN FRANCISCO

CONTOUR
LINES AT 10'

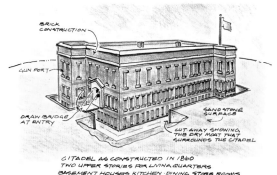

BRICK CONSTRUCTION

GUN PORT

DRAW BRIDGE AT ENTRY

SAND STONE SURFACE

CUT AWAY SHOWING THE DRY MOAT THAT SURROUNDS THE CITADEL

CITADEL AS CONSTRUCTED IN 1860
TWO UPPER STORIES FOR LIVING QUARTERS
BASEMENT HOUSES KITCHEN · DINING STORE ROOMS

as a combination barracks and defensive structure, it had its own water cisterns on the ground, but water, always a problem, had to be brought over from Sausalito, three miles away. New, larger cisterns were built in 1862. The Citadel, built at the summit of the island for strategic reasons, overlooked the fortifications and batteries. (*Figures 10–13*)

Once completed, the silhouette of the red brick Citadel was noticeable throughout the bay, and for nearly fifty years it was the most visible symbol of Alcatraz, except for the lighthouse. Later, the cellblock would have that honor.

Architecture defined and signaled the purpose and function of the island. Once buildings were completed in 1859, access to the island was possible only via the dock and then through the sally port (*Figure 21*), a well-fortified but narrow guardhouse.

Eighty-six men of Company H, Third U.S. Artillery, took command, led by Captain Joseph Stewart, when the fortress was ready.

With the Civil War underway by 1861, Alcatraz was the only site in the Bay Area with permanently mounted guns, eighty-six of them. (*Figures 14–16*) At the same time, Confederate sympathizers thought they might convince the commander of the army's Department of the Pacific to bring the fortress, California, and, of course, its gold into the Confederate cause. The commander of the Pacific, Colonel Albert Johnston, was a Southerner by birth but loyal to the North. In response, he sent ten thousand muskets and 150,000 cartridges to Alcatraz, the primary Union defense post on the West Coast.

Johnston's replacement ordered an immediate full alert of all military personnel in the San Francisco Bay area, increasing

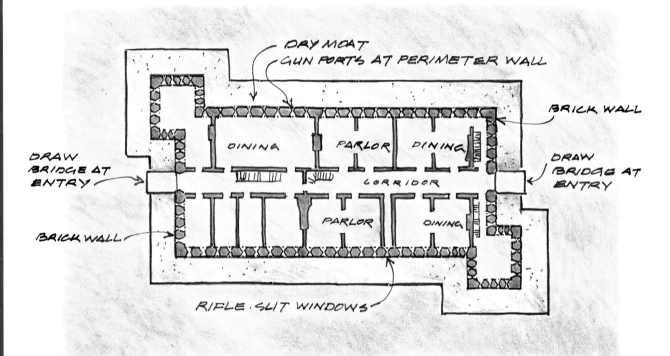

DRY MOAT
GUN PORTS AT PERIMETER WALL

BRICK WALL

DRAW BRIDGE AT ENTRY

DRAW BRIDGE AT ENTRY

DINING

PARLOR

DINING

CORRIDOR

PARLOR

DINING

BRICK WALL

RIFLE SLIT WINDOWS

PLAN OF 2ND LEVEL OF 1860 CITADEL
PLAN OF 3RD LEVEL SIMILAR · BOTH
LEVELS PROVIDE LIVING QUARTERS
FOR 100 SOLDIERS

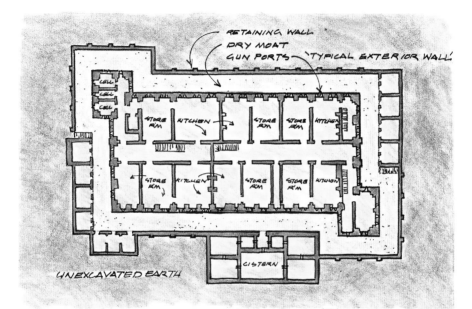

RETAINING WALL
DRY MOAT
GUN PORTS — 'TYPICAL EXTERIOR WALL'

CELL
CELL
CELL

STORE RM   KITCHEN   STORE RM   STORE RM   KITCHEN

STORE RM   KITCHEN   STORE RM   STORE R'M   KITCHEN

UNEXCAVATED EARTH

CISTERN

BASEMENT LEVEL OF 1860 CITADEL
HOUSES·KITCHENS·CELLS AND
STORAGE ROOMS

ROOF LEVEL

3RD LEVEL

2ND LEVEL

DRAW
BRIDGE

DRY
MOAT

BASEMENT
LEVEL

BASEMENT LEVEL STRUCTURE WAS
RETAINED IN THE NEW 1910 CELL BLOCK
THE EXISTING STORE ROOMS BECAME
ISOLATION CELLS

SECTION SHOWING CUT THRU MAIN CORRIDOR.
LIVING UNITS AT BOTH UPPER LEVELS · BASEMENT
STORE ROOMS

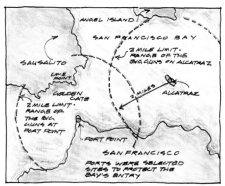

MAP SHOWING THE LOCATION OF THE TWO ARMED PORTS AND THEIR LARGE GUNS FIRING RANGE · FROM A MAP DATED 1863

the complement on Alcatraz to more than 350 by the end of April 1861. New resources appeared, notably the fifteen-inch Rodman cannon, mounted on Alcatraz in 1864, as well as additional soldiers' quarters. Excavation for "bomb-proof" barracks began in 1865; the two-tiered structure was abandoned, however, because of a lack of funds, although one tier was completed, which became the lower level of Building 64 at the dock. (*Figures 17–20*) By 1865, the island had more than one hundred heavy weapons mounted, but no attack on the island occurred.

Almost from its inception as a fort, Alcatraz was a prison. When Captain Stewart arrived in 1859, eleven of his enlisted men were immediately imprisoned in the Sally Port basement, likely for insubordination and drunkenness, becoming the first

inmates. (*Figure 21*) Two months later, Alcatraz received an insane army private for confinement and safekeeping.

The army at this time had neither a prison system nor means of dealing with inmates with long sentences. After 1861, the fortress became the army's first long-term prison, formally designated as a military prison by the Department of the Pacific. During the Civil War, local citizens arrested for treason were confined on the island, as were Confederates from the ship *J.M. Chapman*, joining military prisoners in the guardhouse. Included were two naval officers and two sailors who refused to take an oath of loyalty to the United States at the outbreak of the Civil War. Even the chair of the California Democratic Committee was arrested and sent to Alcatraz for making an incendiary speech during the 1864

SAN FRANCISCO

BAY

15" RODMAN CANNON FACING THE GOLDEN GATE

BRICK WALL OF BATTERY STEVENS

WHEEL FOR CANNON ROTATION

CANNON BALLS

EXAMPLE OF THE BIG GUNS (CANNONS) PLACED ON ALCATRAZ IN 1869 NOTE THE SCALE OF THE SOLDIER NEXT TO THE CANNON

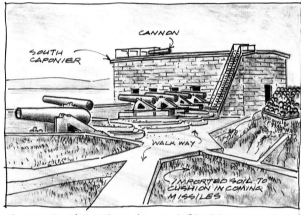

CANNON

SOUTH CAPONIER

WALK WAY

IMPORTED SOIL TO CUSHION INCOMING MISSILES

BATTERY MCCLELLAN FACING SOUTH TOWARDS THE GATE · TYPICAL ISLAND BATTLE STATION · 1864

ENTRANCE TO THE 'BOMB PROOF'
BARRACKS · BUILT IN 1866
NOTE THE FINE BRICKWORK

LIGHT HOUSE

LINE OF PLANNED BUT
UNBUILT STRUCTURE

SALLY PORT

5 FOOT THICK BRICK WALL
GUN PORT

DOCK

UNCOMPLETED 'BOMB PROOF' BARRACKS AT
THE MAIN ISLAND DOCK · CONSTRUCTED 1865-66

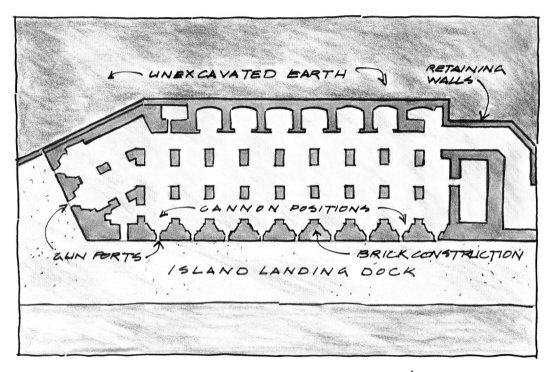

UNEXCAVATED EARTH

RETAINING WALLS

CANNON POSITIONS

GUN PORTS

BRICK CONSTRUCTION

ISLAND LANDING DOCK

FIRST LEVEL OF UNCOMPLETED `BOMB PROOF' BARRACKS   1865-66

VIEW FROM THE DOCKSIDE OF THE 1890's
ISLAND VICTORIAN BUILDINGS

presidential campaign. After posting bond and swearing an oath of allegiance to the Union, he was released.

Soon, the Presidio and other western army posts sent their deserters, escapees, thieves, and drunks to the island, more secure than their own garrison stockades. But Alcatraz was running out of room. The howitzer rooms of the sally port guardhouse were overflowing. The need for new facilities meant building a temporary wooden prison in 1863 just north of the guardhouse, but prisoners feared that it would burn down and they would be trapped. Several adjacent structures called the Lower Prison replaced it, housing an average of one hundred men through the late nineteenth century. By 1868, two wooden, barnlike cell blocks were built on the north side of the guardhouse cantilevered out over the road. Cells were only three and a half by six feet and without beds. Prisoners slept on pallets on the floor.

Labor was part of the punishment for all inmates. Some excavated and built new fortifications and housing; others had daily work details at nearby military posts and returned every night. Difficult or untrustworthy prisoners had either indoor tasks or remained confined to their cells.

The end of the Civil War effectively ended the role of Alcatraz as a harbor defense. The smoothbore cannons on the island were suddenly outdated because new rifled artillery (grooved barrels that impart spin to the projectile) had a longer range and were more accurate and powerful against masonry forts. Rather than acting as defensive protection, the tall masonry walls of Alcatraz were suddenly targets.

BRICK WALLS

WOODEN SHACK

SALLY PORT

ENTRANCE TO THE UPPER PART OF THE ISLAND   BUILT 1857

As the Rock's prison role increased and its defensive importance lessened, by 1900 the army decided the isolation of the island would better suit a full-fledged prison than a fortress. The April 1906 San Francisco earthquake confirmed the island's durability, further recommending it for a prison. The island, of course, felt the tremors, which shook buildings and cracked walls and toppled chimneys. But there was no serious damage. However, the city jail on Broadway was damaged and in the path of a growing firestorm. Action had to be taken. Jailers, assisted by the National Guard, herded 176 prisoners through the streets to Fort Mason, where they were placed on a government launch and taken to the relatively undamaged but crowded cellblocks of Alcatraz. They stayed nine days.

By 1907, a new military prison was planned, and soldier-convicts began to fashion a massive cellhouse and set of support buildings on the summit and slopes. Construction on the new building began in 1908 and was complete by 1912. The new six-hundred-foot-long cellhouse rested on top of the remains of the 1850s Citadel that once crowned the island. When building began, workers tore down the upper two stories of the Citadel but retained its bottom floor and basement, which became the infamous dungeons of the new cellhouse. Considered a marvel of penal technology, it featured one-man cells, steam heat, electric lights, running water, and toilets in each cell. The building used reinforced concrete, unlike its stucco and wood predecessors, and on its completion was supposedly the largest reinforced concrete structure in the world.

Construction, of course, provided its own challenges. One of the most important: waste. The military had an easy solution, however. They simply tossed garbage and anything else not needed directly into the bay or burned it in the incinerator. On occasion, even aging buildings were either reduced to rubble or pushed over the side or used for landfill on the island. Decay, caused by weather and the sea, was constant.

Occasionally, material was reused in newer construction, which was cheaper than bringing in replacements from the mainland. This partly explains the sometimes hodgepodge construction materials and designs. Broken Citadel bricks were mixed into concrete destined for the cellhouse. And interior iron staircases from the Citadel were reinstalled in the new 1912 prison building. Gigantic granite blocks originally designed as gun mounts were reused as the wharf's bulkheads and in retaining walls. Riveted bar doors from nineteenth-century cellblocks were tossed into concrete retaining walls for additional strength. The underground ammunition magazine was converted into an oil storage reservoir. Granite doorways from the Citadel were rebuilt as entrances to the prison. Later, spiral stairs from the cellblocks, renovated in the 1930s, were moved to the wharf and incorporated into the supports for

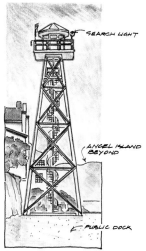

SEARCH LIGHT

ANGEL ISLAND BEYOND

PUBLIC DOCK

GUARD TOWER AT THE DOCK · CIRCA 1940.

the Dock Tower built in 1940. (*Figure 22*) The buried nineteenth-century gun batteries served as foundations for the prison and Industrial Building built along the island's perimeter.

But using recycled material in the construction of the cellhouse created later problems. The prison's walls were reinforced with a web of steel bars that increased the strength of the concrete, but many of them were placed so close to the walls' surface that they began to rust as moisture from the salty air saturated the surface. Mixing the broken brick into the concrete as an economic measure rendered it porous, allowing salty air to penetrate even deeper into the concrete.

As needs changed, elements of the cellhouse were altered as well: An arched colonnade originally marking the front entrance to the new building and forming an attractive open breezeway was eventually enclosed, supposedly for security reasons. Renewal and rebuilding efficiently incorporated older materials, but they were often unsatisfactory and damaged.

CHAPTER 3

ISLAND ARCHITECTURE & THE LIGHTHOUSE

All the iron shutters for the windows have been made and hung, frames set up, and sash put in . . . The main stairs in the hall leading from the basement to the roof (all iron in the soldiers barracks, and iron frame with wooden treads and risers in the Officers Quarters) have [also] been finished. —LIEUTENANT JAMES BIRDSEYE MCPHERSON, 1858–1859 ANNUAL REPORT

Architecturally, the island echoed the mainland, establishing a kind of symbolic bridge stretching one and a quarter miles over open water. (*Figure 30*)

Marking the Victorian style in San Francisco are the many tall and narrow wood-framed homes with gingerbread trim, steeply pitched roofs, gables for dormers, and porches. (*Figure 23*) They sometimes also have second-story balconies, steps to the front door, pointed-arch windows, and scrolled ornamentation. Coastal redwood was often used for the structural members and decorative elements. Alamo Square and Pacific Heights in San Francisco today contain many examples of Victorian buildings. (*Figure 24*)

The Queen Anne style flourished in San Francisco at the end of the nineteenth century as well and can be seen today on homes in the Western Addition neighborhood. Characterizing this style was classical ornamentation combined with medieval forms, shaped shingles, spoolwork, foliated plasterwork, and irregular, gabled, hipped, and conical roofs. (*Figure 25*) Material emphasized varied surface textures, and entrance designs often included porches. A turret or brick chimney might appear,

PACIFIC OCEAN

ANGEL ISLAND

SAN FRANCISCO BAY

VICTORIAN STYLE
BUILDINGS

CANNON

FORT POINT 1886 WITH VICTORIAN STYLE BUILDINGS

SAN FRANCISCO'S · ALAMO SQUARE · VICTORIAN
STYLE BUILDINGS · BUILT IN THE 1890's

Opposite: *Figures 23 & 24*
Below: *Figure 25*

TYPICAL VICTORIAN HOUSE (OF THE 1890'S (QUEEN ANNE STYLE) CAN BE SEEN AT 4128 - 24TH STREET. SAN FRANCISCO

or the popular fish-scale shingles might be featured. A variety of buildings on Alcatraz display these features, from the nineteenth-century Officers' Quarters to storerooms (later torn down).

Between 1849 and 1915 in San Francisco, almost forty-eight thousand homes in the Victorian, Queen Anne, and then Edwardian style were built, marking the growth of the city from the California gold rush to the Panama Pacific International Exposition in 1915. All these styles, grouped under the title "Victorian," began to influence the architecture of private and public institutions, including the standardized building plans of Alcatraz.

The Victorian style defined the early buildings of Alcatraz, even the most fortified. The earliest building incorporating this style on the island was the lighthouse. Built on the south peak, it became the most visible structure on the island, seen from throughout the bay. When the army engineers began to build on Alcatraz, a lighthouse was the priority: Sitting in the middle of the harbor, the island was a hazard to ships, so a warning beacon was an essential navigation aide, ensuring a safe passage through the Golden Gate strait. Completed before the Citadel, it was the very first lighthouse on the West Coast. (*Figures 26–28*)

Construction, however, did not go smoothly. The building went up quickly, but there was a delay with the third-order Fresnel lens to be supplied by a Parisian company, L. Sautier. Shipped from France to New York, the lens then went by boat around Cape Horn before arriving in San Francisco in 1853. The lens consisted of hand-ground crystal prisms set in a brass

CHIMNEY

LIGHT AND LENS

LIVING QUARTERS

CANNON BALLS STORAGE

WEST FACING VIEW OF THE LIGHTHOUSE · NOTE CANNON BALL MOUNDS (BUILT · 1856)

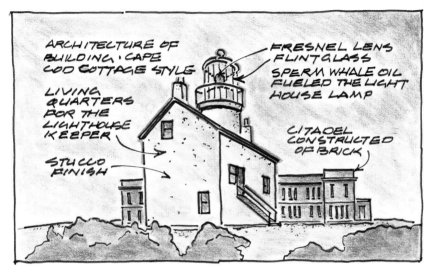

ARCHITECTURE OF
BUILDING · CAPE
COO COTTAGE STYLE

FRESNEL LENS
FLINT GLASS

SPERM WHALE OIL
FUELED THE LIGHT
HOUSE LAMP

LIVING
QUARTERS
FOR THE
LIGHTHOUSE
KEEPER

CITADEL
CONSTRUCTED
OF BRICK

STUCCO
FINISH

SOUTH FACING VIEW OF THE LIGHTHOUSE
CONSTRUCTED IN 1856 · DEMOLISHED IN
1910
• FIRST LIGHTHOUSE CONSTRUCTED ON THE
WEST COAST OF THE UNITED STATES

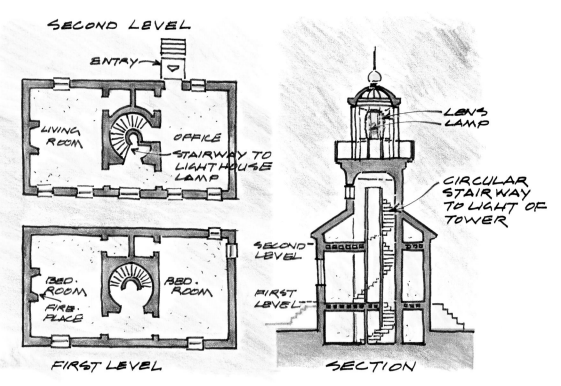

SECOND LEVEL

ENTRY

LIVING ROOM

OFFICE

STAIRWAY TO LIGHTHOUSE LAMP

FIRST LEVEL

BED ROOM

BED ROOM

FIRE PLACE

SECTION

LENS LAMP

CIRCULAR STAIRWAY TO LIGHT OF TOWER

SECOND LEVEL

FIRST LEVEL

PLANS AND SECTION OF LIGHTHOUSE
THIS ILLUSTRATION TAKEN FROM A BLUEPRINT
DATED 1854

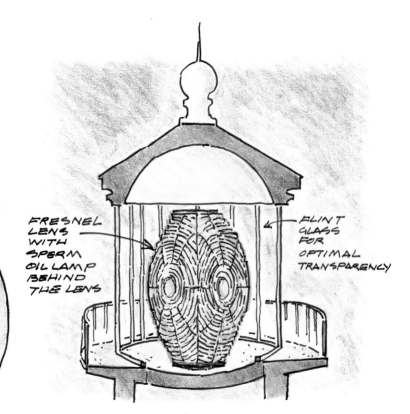

CROSS SECTION OF A FRESNEL LENS SIMILAR TO AN AUTOMOBILE HEADLIGHT LENS

CROSS SECTION OF A CONVENTIONAL CONVEX LENS OF THE EQUIVALENT POWER TO THE FRESNEL LENS

FRESNEL LENS WITH SPERM OIL LAMP BEHIND THE LENS

FLINT GLASS FOR OPTIMAL TRANSPARENCY

CUTAWAY SECTION OF LIGHTHOUSE LIGHT · 1856

frame that could focus a steady beam of light from a whale-oil flame visible for some nineteen miles (car headlights today still incorporate features of the Fresnel lens). (*Figure 29*)

Finding a contractor to install the apparatus took almost another year, but finally at sunset on June 1, 1854, the first lighthouse

VICTORIAN STYLE OFFICERS QUARTERS ON THE EAST SIDE OF THE ISLAND 1893

keeper, Michael Cassin, lit the lamp in the forty-foot lighthouse tower for the first time. The circular balcony surrounding the lantern room provided a uniform silhouette to the tower, while allowing the keepers to regularly inspect the lantern and its function. The Fresnel lens, which some navigators said looked too much like a streetlight, would operate until 1902, when a flashing lens replaced the steady light. Throughout the earthquake of 1906, the light continued to operate with only minor damage to its tower.

Upon the lighthouse's completion in 1854, two federal agencies now competed over the island: The Lighthouse Board controlled the light, the War Department the Citadel. Occasionally, commanding officers would complain that the grounds of the lighthouse station were too domestic and detracted from the military look of the post. The building had a neat, compact appearance, even when surrounded by rows of cannonballs stacked three and four high. Additions and expansions to the lighthouse cottage took place throughout the 1890s, and a post office was soon located in the basement. When a former sailor, Captain Leeds, took over the lighthouse, he put up lattice fencing, planted flowerbeds, and kept the buildings whitewashed. The compact wood and stucco building, with its short, if not stubby, tower above the living quarters, functioned effectively until 1908. (*Figure 28*)

By 1908, the War Department began construction of a new concrete cellhouse on top of the island. (*Figures 32–33*) The lighthouse would have to be moved because the walls of the completed prison would rise higher than the lantern, cutting visibility of the lens by 50 percent. On December 1, 1909, the lens was moved into the new tower and relit. (*Figures 35–36*) Demolition of the original 1854 building occurred in 1912. And by 1939, coast guard personnel replaced civilian keepers; by 1963, the lighthouse became an automated station, the light evolving from whale oil to kerosene to electricity. In 1970, during the American Indian Occupation, the lighthouse burned down; only the concrete tower survived. Restored and renovated at the end of the occupation, and later enlarged, the lighthouse is still in operation—the oldest continually operating lighthouse in the west.

CHAPTER 4

FROM FORTRESS TO PRISON

The prisoners are crazed with fear every time any unusual outside noise is made at night, fearing fire and that they will be burned to death.

—QUARTERMASTER REPORT, JANUARY 1902

Although the army decided in the early 1900s that Alcatraz was no longer needed to defend San Francisco from naval invasion, they nevertheless continued to see its value as a prison. Between 1903 and 1905, Alcatraz held 461 convicts, although most were imprisoned for two years or less. By 1907, however, the role of Alcatraz formally changed: The War Department dropped the island's designation as a harbor defense fort and would enlarge the site as a permanent prison for the U.S. Army. It would also construct a new cellhouse, partly necessary because

of a large influx of U.S. soldiers convicted of crimes in the Philippines. In 1909, the brick Citadel was torn down, but the entire first floor of the building, below ground level, remained as a basement and foundation floor. The now darkened space would briefly serve for solitary confinement. (*Figure 32*)

By 1915, the term "prison" became unfashionable; replacing it was "disciplinary barracks," along with a new emphasis on rehabilitation. That year Alcatraz was officially renamed U.S. Disciplinary Barracks, Pacific Branch, and would remain a military prison until 1934 when it became the maximum-security facility U.S. Penitentiary Alcatraz.

Designed by Major Reuben B. Turner, the first commandant of the military prison, the scale of the new cellhouse was, for its time, immense, incorporating a mess hall, hospital, administration facilities, and of course cellblock. One important design feature was that each cellblock stood separate from the others, with barred windows. The new building also established a centralized work space, a new utility system, and a set of concrete buildings to replace the original wooden structures. (*Figure 33*)

Turner wanted to harmonize the buildings planned to accommodate the island's new role by duplicating the popular mission revival style of the mainland and the new lighthouse. The California missions the Franciscans built informed the style, which included such characteristics as arched openings, pastel stucco over wood construction, clay-tile roofs, exposed rafters, mock bell towers, quatrefoil windows, and usually an arcade along one or more sides. (*Figures 31 and 34–39*)

FORT MASON POST CHAPEL · EXAMPLE OF MISSION REVIVAL STYLE CONSTRUCTED IN 1942

The morgue, a small building just down from the cellhouse, was one of the simplest expressions of the mission revival style on Alcatraz (though it was never used during the military years as a morgue; dead bodies of soldiers and prisoners were sent over to Angel Island). (*Figure 41*) Another example was the warden's house, originally built for the post commandant in the 1920s. (*Figure 40*) Its two-and-half-story structure with its curved gables was noticeable from most points on the island. Well-behaved inmates acted as stewards, cooks, and gardeners for the warden and his family. The house stood until it was destroyed by fire in 1970 during the American Indian Occupation.

NORTH ELEVATION OF THE CITADEL BUILT IN 1860 SUPERIMPOSED ON NORTH ELEVATION
OF THE MAIN CELL BLOCK BUILT IN 1910

DRY
MOAT
BASEMENT RETAINED FOR
THE CELL HOUSE · DUNGEONS

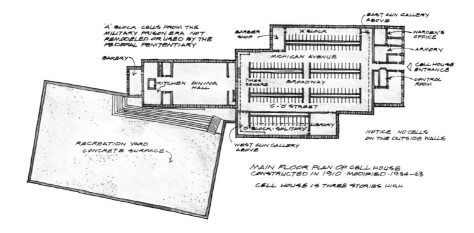

'A' BLOCK · CELLS FROM THE
MILITARY PRISON ERA · NOT
REMODELED OR USED BY THE
FEDERAL PENITENTIARY

EAST GUN GALLERY
ABOVE

BARBER
SHOP

'A' BLOCK

WARDEN'S
OFFICE

BAKERY

ARMORY

MICHIGAN AVENUE

CELL HOUSE
ENTRANCE

KITCHEN DINING
HALL

TIMES
SQUARE

BROADWAY

CONTROL
ROOM

C · D STREET

RECREATION YARD
CONCRETE SURFACE

'D' BLOCK · SOLITARY

LIBRARY

NOTICE · NO CELLS
ON THE OUTSIDE WALLS

WEST GUN GALLERY
ABOVE

MAIN FLOOR PLAN OF CELL HOUSE
CONSTRUCTED IN 1910 · MODIFIED · 1934-63

CELL HOUSE IS THREE STORIES HIGH

FORT SCOTT BARRACKS IN THE PRESIDIO
ARCHITECTURE MISSION REVIVAL

PRESENT BEACON LIGHT TOWER AND
HOUSE AS IT EXISTED TILL 1970.
CONSTRUCTED FOR THREE FAMILIES.
MISSION REVIVAL BUILT IN 1909

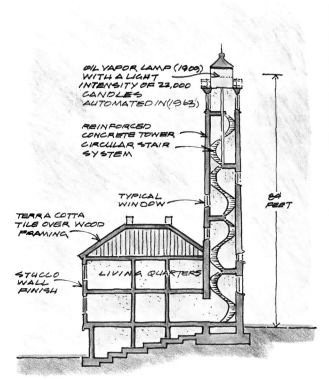

OIL VAPOR LAMP (1909) WITH A LIGHT INTENSITY OF 22,000 CANDLES AUTOMATED IN (1963)

REINFORCED CONCRETE TOWER CIRCULAR STAIR SYSTEM

TYPICAL WINDOW

84 FEET

TERRA COTTA TILE OVER WOOD FRAMING

STUCCO WALL FINISH

LIVING QUARTERS

BUILDING SECTION THRU THE PRESENT LIGHTHOUSE · MISSION REVIVAL · CONSTRUCTED IN 1909

REINFORCED CONCRETE WALLS

BUILDING 77 IS A MISSION REVIVAL ARCHITECTURAL STYLE CONSTRUCTED IN THE 1920s · IT HAS HOUSED A MILITARY CHAPEL · SCHOOL AND LIVING QUARTERS

MODERN PUBLIC FACILITIES AT THE DOCK
DESIGNED IN THE MISSION REVIVAL STYLE
BY MACDONALD ARCHITECTS FOR THE
GOLDEN GATE NATIONAL PARK ASSOCIATION

POST EXCHANGE AND OFFICERS CLUB ·
MISSION REVIVAL ARCHITECTURE · 1910

The silhouette of the island soon changed. The island lost its rounded, hilly form, replaced by the square corners and high walls of the cellhouse and exercise yard. A powerhouse smokestack and new lighthouse tower soon gave the appearance of a ship's masts on either side of the main prison building. To many, the Rock took on the look of an ocean liner. (*Figure 42*)

Despite the regimented look of the prison, prisoners during this time did not wear striped convict's uniforms, and they appeared curiously disarrayed for a military complex. A large *P* on the back of the shirts, jackets, and hats of their obsolete military uniforms identified the military prisoners. When nineteen Hopi Indians were incarcerated in 1895 for refusing to send their children to a non-native school, they were ordered to wear military uniforms. A photo from 1903 at the noon count shows a lineup of inmates in a variety of cast-off uniforms dating back to the Indian Wars of 1866–1890.

In October 1933, U.S. Attorney General Homer Cummings announced on radio that the government would build a new prison on Alcatraz Island for convicts with "advanced degrees in crime." When the army deactivated the military facility, most of the prisoners transferred to either the federal prison in Leavenworth, Kansas, or Fort Jay in New Jersey. But thirty-two of the worst offenders remained behind, now in the care of the Bureau of Prisons and the new warden, James A. Johnston. Alcatraz had become America's first maximum-security prison.

REINFORCED
CONCRETE WALLS

PRISON WARDEN'S HOUSE · MISSION REVIVAL ·
CONSTRUCTED IN 1929

The prison would symbolize the determination of the federal government to reestablish law and order in American society. Isolated in the middle of the bay, seemingly on exhibit, would be criminals of "the vicious and irredeemable type." And in their individual cells, their "evil influence" would not extend to others.

The public and the press embraced the idea. An escape-proof prison for the worst criminals in the country, a prison devoted to punishment, satisfied the need for protection against violence. San Franciscans, including the police chief, objected, however, saying that it would bring dangerous criminals in close proximity to the general population, and that the prison would dominate the views of many

MORGUE AS BUILT IN MISSION REVIVAL STYLE 1910

surrounding the bay. The new Golden Gate Bridge, then under construction, would create enough issues since it would soon facilitate daily population increases in the city. But the Justice Department and the Bureau of Prisons went ahead anyway. The *San Francisco Chronicle* published editorials opposing it, pointing out for example that some twenty-three military prisoners had escaped over the years. Instead of a prison, a peace statue should be erected on the island, a 1934 article argued. A government press release tried to combat objections, stressing the best techniques of modern penology, while appealing to the city's sense of patriotism. Alcatraz would give the citizens the chance "to cooperate in a patriotic

SILHOUETTE OF ALCATRAZ ISLAND VIEWED
FROM RUSSIAN HILL

SILHOUETTE OF AN OCEANLINER SHOWING
WHY ALCATRAZ IS REFERRED TO AS A SHIP
IN THE SAN FRANCISCO BAY

and public-spirited manner in the Government's campaign against the criminal."

Alcatraz, said the government, would have unprecedented security, (*Figure 22*) isolate its inmates from the outside world, and restrict their opportunities for interaction with each other. All prisoners would be treated the same regardless of notoriety or prestige. And the Justice Department's requirements for the prison were high: Escape was to be virtually impossible, there should be no opportunities to create violence of any sort, no business could be conducted from the prison, no special privileges would exist, information flow would be strictly controlled, and there would be "real punishment." The Bureau of Prisons summarized this as a "maximum-security, minimum-privilege" institution. To this end, all administrative personnel were required to live on the island. And no press would be permitted access, essentially shutting down publicity for the numerous high-profile inmates to be housed there, although they comprised less than 1 percent of the entire federal prison population.

Alcatraz operated in secret. The public did not know what really went on at the most fearsome prison in America, and they were curious. But they could only stare from a distance (*Figure 43*) or read the sensational stories the papers featured. Dungeons? Torture? Murders? These were all suppositions that fed the public imagination soon expanded by the movies. The secrecy surrounding the prison only intensified the public's desire to know more.

Warden James A. Johnston, a former lawyer, banker, head of Folsom State Prison, and warden at San Quentin, installed new security: elevated gun galleries at the end of the cellhouse,

VIEWING ALCATRAZ FROM FISHERMAN'S WHARF (1946)

electronically controlled gates and doors, metal detectors, tear-gas canisters in the ceiling of the dining hall, (*Figures 44–45*) barbed wire atop a cyclone fence that encircled the prison, and warning signs on all four sides of the island ordering boats to stay at least two hundred yards away. And where most prisons had one guard for every ten convicts, Johnston hired one for every three Alcatraz prisoners. He also ordered twelve official counts a day, with random and unofficial counts occurring at a moment's notice.

BARRACKS BUILDING 64 AT THE DOCK · 1934 · AT THE BEGINNING OF THE FEDERAL PRISON ERA

But Johnston, who had improved conditions at Folsom Prison and San Quentin, also took steps to make Alcatraz more hospitable. He made sure the food (*Figures 46–49*) was decent, and inmates could take as much as they wanted as long as they ate

everything. Realizing that the grayness was the greatest complaint—not the wind, cold, or isolation—Johnston had larger prison spaces painted in lively colors. He also experimented with colors inside cells, believing that dark green for the back wall and light green for the side walls would make the cell look bigger than if it was all white. In later years, cells came to have checkered floors, patterned walls, and even stripes.

Sections of the cellhouse had nicknames. Facing west was "Sunset Strip," home to D Block and its thirty-six isolation cells and six solitary confinement cells. C Block ("Park Avenue") and B Block were behind, long rows of cells separated by "Broadway" that ended to the north at "Times Square," the corridor beneath

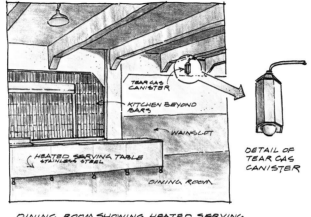

DINING ROOM SHOWING HEATED SERVING
TABLE AND KITCHEN BARRED AREA

a large clock and entranceway to the dining hall. Cellblocks ran in a northwest direction with cells facing either east or west. Two gun galleries were at either end of the cellblocks so guards could observe the walkways and aisles. Guards in the galleries were armed, although officers did not carry arms in the cellhouse itself. At the west end of the cellblock was the dining room, which guards, tear gas canisters in the ceiling, and a strict routine secured. (*Figure 50*)

The first prisoners—fifty-three in all—arrived on the night of August 22, 1934, sent from Atlanta in specially designed prison railcars. In Tiburon, California, the cars were placed on barges and towed to the island. Al Capone, bootlegger and gangster and Alcatraz prisoner No. 85, arrived in the first shipment.

Though he was sentenced to ten years for tax evasion, AZ 85 ("AZ" the official designation of Alcatraz prisoners, taken from the last two letters of "Alcatraz") was especially worrisome. On his prison record card under "Criminal Specialty" it read "Hoodlum," but he was generally cooperative and even played banjo in the Rock Islanders, the prison band, which gave regular Sunday concerts. The first prisoner was Frank Bolt, a transfer from the military prison. Sentenced to five years, he had only three months and six days left to serve when he became AZ 1. After the first prisoners arrived and were in their cells, Warden Johnston sent an arranged telegram to Attorney General Homer Cummings, which read "fifty-three crates of

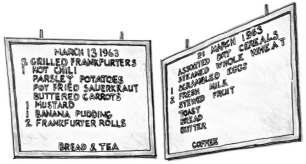

MARCH 13 1963
2 GRILLED FRANKFURTERS
1 HOT CHILI
  PARSLEY POTATOES
  POT FRIED SAUERKRAUT
  BUTTERED CARROTS
1 MUSTARD
1 BANANA PUDDING
2 FRANKFURTER ROLLS

BREAD & TEA

21 MARCH 1963
ASSORTED DRY CEREALS
STEAMED WHOLE WHEAT
1 SCRAMBLED EGGS
2 FRESH MILK
  STEWED FRUIT
  TOAST
  BREAD
  BUTTER

COFFEE

DINNER MENU   BREAKFAST MENU
TYPICAL PRISONER'S MEAL MENU
APPLIED DURING THE FEDERAL PERIOD 1934-63

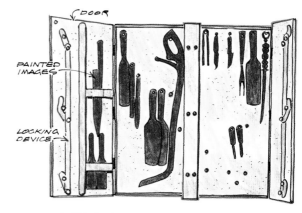

DOOR

PAINTED
IMAGES

LOCKING
DEVICE

LOCKED CABINET FOR KITCHEN UTENSILS
WALL HUNG

Opposite: Figures 46 & 47
Below: Figures 48 & 49

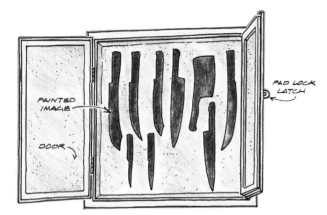

PAINTED IMAGE

DOOR

PAD LOCK LATCH

LOCKED CABINET FOR KITCHEN KNIVES

GLASS BLOCKS

GLASSED IN CENTRALIZED KITCHEN OBSERVATION STATION

furniture from Atlanta received in good condition—installed—no breakage."

The first prisoners were later joined by George "Machine Gun" Kelly, escape artist Roy Gardner, and murderer Robert Stroud (the "Birdman of Alcatraz"), all sent

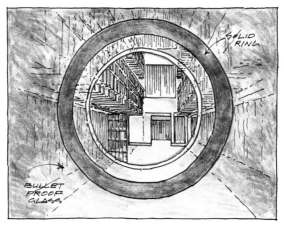

VIEW DOWN BROADWAY GUN PORT

from Leavenworth. Despite Stroud's nickname, he was never allowed to keep birds on Alcatraz—he had them earlier at Leavenworth prison. But he spent years working and publishing two books on bird illnesses: *Diseases of Canaries* (1933), the first pet disease book published in America, and *Stroud's Digest on the Diseases of Birds* (1944). In *Birdman of Alcatraz*, Burt Lancaster portrayed Stroud as gentle and misunderstood; in reality Stroud was a violent and antisocial psychotic disliked by prisoners and

guards alike. After his transfer to Alcatraz in 1942, Stroud spent six years in solitary in D Block and eleven years in an isolated cell in the prison's hospital. (*Figure 52*) He died on November 23, 1963, the day after the assassination of John F. Kennedy.

After a shower, many of the new prisoners would be marched naked down Broadway between B and C Blocks to deflate their egos. At their cells—there were 270 in all—they were issued coveralls and a copy of the strict Institution Rules and Regulations.

All aspects of prison life were strictly regulated. Regulation 28 mandated that "caps are not worn inside the cellhouse at any time." Inmates could smoke in their cells but in few other locations, and the regulations prohibited loud talking, loitering, or

A · 12 BOOKS (MAX.)
B · PERSONAL PAPERS
C · PAINT BOX
D · HEAD PHONES
E · ASH TRAY
F · SOAP
G · MIRROR
H · TOOTHPOWDER
I · RAZOR
J · SHAVING BRUSH
K · SHAVING MUG
L · DRINKING CUP
M · FACE TOWEL
N · BATHROBE
O · RAIN COAT
P · CALENDAR
Q · COAT + CAP
R · SOAP
S · SINK STOPPER
T · CLEANING POWDER
U · TOILET PAPER
V · SHOES
W · MUSICAL INSTRUMENT
X · BROOM
Y · BASKET
Z · BLANKETS

FEDERAL REGULATION
CELL FOR INMATES
NOTE · MANDATORY PLACEMENT OF ITEMS

visiting on the galleries. The first rule required each prisoner to keep his "cell neat, clean and free from contraband," and a diagram on page 8 showed prisoners how to keep their cells orderly, illustrating the meticulous placement of items on the two shelves and around a bed. (*Figure 51*) Any dangerous articles such as narcotics, weapons, or money would result in disciplinary action and a possible trip to court. A property card listing the inmate's personal items had to be filled out and kept above the cell door behind the locking mechanism.

All inmates wore the same uniform: a blue chambray shirt, blue and white trousers with a web waist belt, and standard-issue shoes. The belt was to be worn with the prisoner's registration number in plain view in the center of the back. Alcatraz's inmates never wore striped prison uniforms.

The penal philosophy of Alcatraz was simple: No man was directly sentenced to the island. He "earned" his way there if he was a security risk at another federal prison or was disruptive. A convict also earned his way off, but only to another federal penitentiary. The idea? No man would ever be paroled directly from Alcatraz. On occasion, however, some were released from the island if they had finished their sentences. Studies of 975 return-to-prison records of Alcatraz inmates show that only 37 percent of men labeled as "habitual" offenders returned to prison; nearly two-thirds remained free.

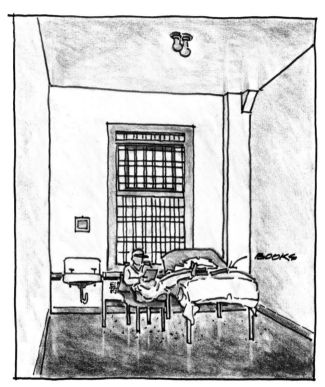

ILLUSTRATION DRAWN FROM
A PHOTO OF STROUD SEATED
IN HIS HOSPITAL CELL ROOM

Prisoners had some limited privileges, however. Alcatraz was the place where you could smoke more than you could talk. Johnston had issued a silence rule for the cellhouse and dining hall, but he also gave every man three packs of cigarettes per week. There were also tobacco dispensers in the cellblocks; if you ran short, you could roll your own. This deprived cigarettes of their usual prison currency value and reduced the use of tobacco as a bribe. But it gave rise to a peculiar Alcatraz habit: Gambling debts were paid in push-ups—sixty for a lost game of dominos, six hundred (in installments) for a wrong guess on the World Series.

Recreation for the inmates consisted largely of softball, handball, volleyball, and—surprisingly—bridge. Bridge players sat in special corners in the recreation area that were protected from the wind. Using specifically marked dominoes on a special board, the bridge players sat on cotton-stuffed cushions playing on small tables. A former inmate, Jim Quillen, reported that

"Culbertson's Beginners Book of Bridge was beyond a doubt the most desired and read book in the prison's [history]." "Blackwood convention," "finesse," "grand slam," "no trump," and "bid" were terms known to almost every inmate, Quillen added. Inmates did not visit the prison's library: they would choose three books at a time from a list that was in their cells, and the books came to them. Staff members carefully selected titles to add to the library, which was actually a holdover from the army period. In 1933 it held several thousand books; by 1960 it contained fifteen thousand. Every prisoner had a library card.

How long did inmates stay on Alcatraz? Five years was the usual, although the length of a convict's stay was officially open-ended. Inmates were sequestered on Alcatraz until they stopped being troublemakers, then they were transferred back to their old prisons. Over the twenty-nine years that Alcatraz operated as a federal penitentiary, the highest number of prisoners at one time was 342, the lowest 222. The total number imprisoned was 1,547.

CHAPTER 5

———

ESCAPES

Go ahead—swim! —COLONEL G. MAURAY CRALLE,
COMMANDANT OF ALCATRAZ, 1926

In the early days of the federal prison and in an effort to hinder escape, Warden Johnston required inmates to change their cells on a regular basis. Keys were the most highly guarded items; the most important dangled from heavy twine and were lowered to officers on the cell floor below via pulleys. (*Figure 53*) Even the keys of boat captains were kept in a tower at the dock, hoisted up on a cable until the boat was ready to depart.

Meant to punish unruly prisoners rather than rehabilitate them, Alcatraz structured the formerly undisciplined lives of inmates. San Francisco's shore, a little more than a mile away, let the prisoners see what they were missing every day.

Reinforcing the enticing aroma from the Ghirardelli Chocolate factory was the huge, lit Ghirardelli sign, which could be seen from the island. If the wind was right, the inmates would also often hear music from the yacht club parties held at the nearby marinas. Recreation on the island was limited: Books and magazines, when available, were censored, current events cut out. An inmate could write and receive letters, but they, too, were heavily edited. Activities in the yard were also curtailed to a couple of hours on Sundays. And there was no commissary at which to purchase personal items.

Combined with the strict rules and few privileges, life was miserable for all inmates, making Alcatraz the toughest and most feared penitentiary in the country. It is understandable, then, that escape attempts were frequent, but none were successful—although several inmates disappeared, never to be found. In all, there were fourteen attempts involving thirty-six men, the first in 1936 by Joseph Bowers. While on a garbage detail,

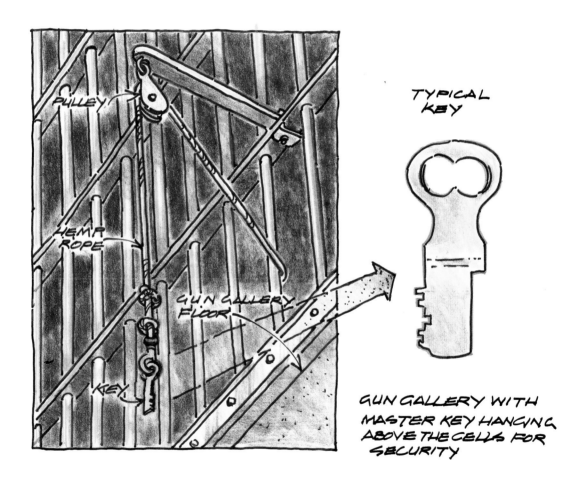

PULLEY

HEMP
ROPE

GUN GALLERY
FLOOR

KEY

TYPICAL
KEY

GUN GALLERY WITH
MASTER KEY HANGING
ABOVE THE CELLS FOR
SECURITY

Opposite: Figure 53
Below: Figure 54

1934
DATE CIVILIAN
PRISONERS
FIRST PLACED
ON THE ISLAND

STYLE OP
THE FIRE
ENGINE
PLACED ON
THE ISLAND

ALCATRAZ ISLAND FIREMAN'S
JACKET PATCH

he climbed up a fence in full view of guards and was shot dead. His fellow convicts called it suicide. (*Figure 55*) Prisoners were also told there were sharks in the waters, hence the "Go ahead—swim" challenge. The claim was false. (*Figure 56*)

TARGET PRACTICE RANGE
LOCATED ABOVE THE OLD SALLY PORT

The most violent escape attempt occurred in May 1946, the failed effort leading to a riot. (*Figure 57*) With four accomplices, a fifth convict succeeded in breaking into the gun gallery. With a rifle and a .45 automatic pistol, they thought they could blast out, but a jammed door and unhelpful hostages prevented their escape. When one of the would-be escapees lost control and shot a series of guards who had been rustled into two cells, the orderly escape began to unravel, although the press still played up the danger. The May 4, 1946, *San Francisco Chronicle* headline read CONVICTS HOLDING OUT; 3RD DAY'S FIGHT AHEAD. The subhead was equally disturbing: CONVICTS REJECT SURRENDER TERMS AFTER ASKING "DEAL"; GUARDS FIRE THROUGH ROOF.

Spectators watched the excitement from the shore through telescopes as navy and coast guard launches circled the island. With his own well-armed guards unable to overcome the most violent escapees, now barricaded, the warden called the marines, and a contingent landed, laying siege to the cellhouse. Using rifle-fired grenades against the sides of the concrete walls, they attacked the cell building, climbed to the roof, and threw demolition and fragmentation grenades through vents and skylights. The island's fire control was very minimal at the time with only one fire truck in service, which helped to put out fires following

THE MAIN TRANSPORTATION· "GENERAL
COXE" BOAT TO THE ISLAND WAS IN
OPERATION UNTIL THE EARLY 1960S

one of the largest escape attempts from the prison. (*Figure 54*) Terrorized convicts in D block retreated to their cells behind mattresses, while three of the ringleaders sought refuge in a service corridor. An assault team finally flushed them out after two and a half days, although when they ultimately entered the small corridor, they found all three holdouts had died from the fusillade. Three fellow conspirators would stand trial: two were executed at San Quentin, while the third, only nineteen, received life in prison. The events made international headlines.

Perhaps the most well-known escape attempt occurred in 1962, involving Allen West, Frank Lee Morris, and the Anglin brothers, John and Clarence. For six months, they constructed an inflatable raft from plastic raincoats. With stolen tools, they chipped through vents in their cells, replacing them with cardboard replicas. They placed papier-mâché heads on their beds to trick the guards and climbed up into a utility corridor in B Block. They crawled along a ventilator shaft, cut through the bars of a vent, and made it to the roof, before clambering down a stovepipe. They headed to the shore past the water tower and power plant and disappeared into the bay. Personal effects but no bodies were found, and the Bureau of Prisons presumed them dead. Clint Eastwood's *Escape from Alcatraz* (1979) was based on their adventure.

Inmate protests occurred occasionally, with most uprisings taking the form of hunger or work strikes. Strikes were the most powerful weapon prison inmates had at Alcatraz. If the Alcatraz inmates didn't go to work, the army's laundry

GUARDS PROTECTING THE DOCK
DURING THE 1946 RIOT

SOLITARY CONFINEMENT CELLS IN THE MAIN CELL BLOCK

didn't get clean and the contracted manufacturing quotas for furniture, gloves, raincoats, brooms, and mats weren't met. Before long, the Alcatraz warden would start getting phone calls from his

ANTI·AIRCRAFT GUN ON TOP OF CELL BLOCK
1942

superiors in Washington. On January 20, 1936, a strike began in the laundry room to protest the rigid rules, and extra guards appeared with gas bombs. The walkout began when six men left their work assignments and walked down the stairs to the door of the laundry room. They clapped their hands, and sixty-eight other inmates joined them. Their number soon increased to 101. But the protest did not last.

The miserable conditions that drove some inmates to protest and others to attempt escape soon came under public scrutiny. Myths about Alcatraz, from interrogations to torture, persisted throughout the prison years. Enforced silence and the use of a "dungeon" began to be viewed as not only ineffective but also harsh. At first, Alcatraz operated under an effective shroud of secrecy, but by the late 1930s, both the public and its elected representatives began to hear stories about Alcatraz from released inmates, and they wanted changes.

Two views of Alcatraz began to emerge at the end of the 1930s and the beginning of the 1940s: one, via rumor-based sensational stories, cast a negative light on prison policies and administration; the other, supported by newspapers, was that Alcatraz embodied a get-tough-on-crime attitude. Was Alcatraz the answer to one of the nation's major social problems or a sign of systematic failures to confront crime? A November 1937

Philadelphia Inquirer headline read RIOTS AND BLOODSHED ARE FORECAST AT ALCATRAZ: CONVICTS CAN'T WIN BUT SILENCE IS WORSE THAN MACHINE GUNS; THE ROCK A BARREL OF DYNAMITE WITH TOUGH WARDEN SITTING ON THE LID. Alcatraz itself was being put on trial.

In 1939, a new attorney general, Frank Murphy, wanted improvements at the Rock (naming Alcatraz the "Rock" originated in the 1940s with the soldiers who served on the island as part of an anti-aircraft post during WWII [*Figure 59*]). Murphy declared that "the whole institution is conducive to psychology that builds up a sinister and vicious attitude among the prisoners." But rather than let it be closed down, Warden Johnston eased the rule of silence in the cellblock, and the Public Works Administration pumped more than $1 million into a facilities-upgrade program. Much of that money was used to remodel D Block into a high-security isolation area called the Treatment Unit. (*Figure 58*) After 1940, and especially after Warden Johnston

retired in 1948, conditions for the Alcatraz inmates continued to improve: they received additional recreation time, radio access, and more magazines, as well as art supplies, and movies twice a month.

CHAPTER 6

LIFE
ON THE
ROCK

America needs an isolated penal colony if it is ever to shake off the tentacles of the crime octopus.

—*REAL DETECTIVE*, JANUARY 1934

Contradicting the image of the impregnable fortress housing the most dangerous felons in America, who underwent deserving if grueling punishment, was day-to-day life on the Rock. During the federal prison period (1934–1963), sixty guard families and ten bachelor guards lived on the island. There were almost seventy children residing with the families, in apartments a quarter of a mile below the cellhouse. The kids played on abandoned military cannons and hung out in the canteen, post office, and bowling alley. The family apartment building, built in the early 1940s, brought comfort, but in the early years, families had no telephones and had to hike to the prison office to make or receive calls. The end of summer meant a watermelon festival on the dock; Christmas Eve was spent caroling around the island.

On holidays, families were permitted inside the prison theatre to view the same G-rated movie the prisoners had seen that afternoon, although by the 1940s, movies started to be shown in the social hall. Families and children also enjoyed the notoriety of being on the island with America's most hardened criminals. "Al Capone used to deliver our milk" one mother mistakenly reported. Another resident described the well-dressed Mrs. Capone riding out alone on the launch to visit her husband, leaving her chauffer and bodyguards behind. Prisoners sought to befriend the kids, recovering balls, wishing them happy birthday, and on one occasion giving a nine-year-old a baseball glove that was being thrown away. Less dangerous criminals cut children's hair and cooked, cleaned, and on occasion babysat.

ALCATRAZ TRANSPORT BOAT "MCDOWELL".
50' LONG. USED IN THE 1930S TO THE 1940S
FOR CONVEYING GOODS AND PEOPLE TO THE
ISLAND

Of greater danger, perhaps, were reporters. They would often wait for the children to get off the boat for school in San Francisco and would pepper them with questions. (*Figures 60–63*) Most ignored the queries, but occasionally one child would describe a dungeon on the island where criminals survived on bread and water, a total fabrication, of course. The children soon realized the papers would print anything and began to make up incidents and describe nonexistent parts of the prison.

Despite the rather placid coexistence of convicts and civilians on the island, public fear of escapes and riots increased, owing in part to the emergence of films about Alcatraz. This began in 1937 with a series of movies focusing on dangerous inmates, their violent behavior, and constant escape attempts: *The Last Gangster*, *Alcatraz Island*, *King of Alcatraz*, and *Prison Train* were all released between 1937 and 1938. They contained such memorable lines as *The Last Gangster*'s "There she is, boys. You're gonna snuggle in the arms of Alcatraz. If you ever hit a tougher stir, it'll be when you step out of your coffin," and *Alcatraz Island*'s "I've heard of some tough cans, but I guess this joint beats them all." Designed to instill confidence in the security of the prison, the films had the opposite effect: apprehension followed by anxiety.

Details of life on Alcatraz were not publicly known, so Hollywood could exploit legends, mysteries, and fanciful tales. The opening line of the 1937 hit *Alcatraz Island*—"America's

BOAT SCHEDULE

EFFECTIVE · OCTOBER 11, 1959

Leaving Alcatraz

Weekly	Saturday	Sunday	Holiday
A.M.	A.M.	A.M.	A.M.
12:10	12:10	12:10	12:10
6:40	7:05	7:05	7:05
7:20	8:10	8:10	8:10
8:10	9:00	9:00	9:00
10:00	10:00	10:00	10:00
	11:00	11:00	11:00
P.M.	P.M.	P.M.	P.M.
12:45	12:45	12:45	12:45
3:20	3:20	3:20	3:20
3:55	4:55	4:55	4:55
4:40	5:40	5:40	5:40
5:10	7:00	7:00	7:00
5:40	8:45	8:45	8:45
7:00	10:00	10:00	10:00
8:45	11:15	11:15	11:15
10:00			
11:15			

(Reverse Side Leaving Ft. Mason)

MAIN BOAT TRANSPORT TO THE ISLAND
NAMED AFTER JAMES JOHNSON, WARDEN
FROM 1934-1948

Opposite: Figure 62
Below: Figure 63

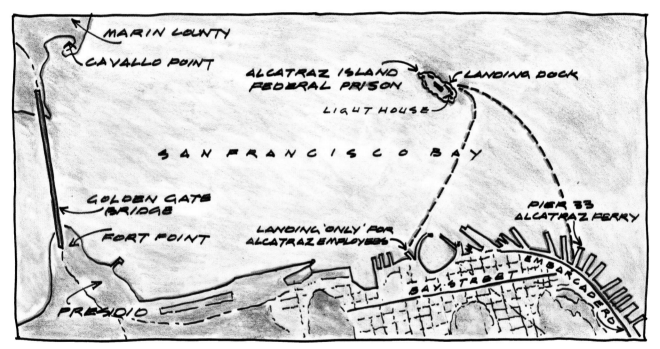

LOCATION OF ALCATRAZ ISLAND IN THE SAN FRANCISCO BAY AREA

penal fortress, grim and mysterious as its name, where cold steel and rushing tides protect civilization from its enemies"—set the tone of public perception of the institution. *Experiment Alcatraz*, the 1950 film that linked the federal penitentiary to military experiments, played on the idea of scientific research. The plot? Five lifers agree to undergo atomic radiation treatment in exchange for their freedom—if they survive. Their exposure results in extreme behavior, but they gain their freedom.

Even after its federal penitentiary days of hardened gangsters, Alcatraz continued to fascinate moviemakers as much as viewers. *The Rock*, starring Sean Connery and Nicolas Cage, became the most expensive film ever made there ($75 million)

THE GLOBAL PEACE CENTER

and was one of the most popular. It was also the only movie to actually premiere at the prison, with a special screening taking place on June 3, 1996, four days before its national release. A complete theatre was built in the prisoner's recreation yard and a carpeted dining hall hosted a sit-down dinner preceded by tours of the prison. The success of the after-hours event contributed to the establishment of night tours of the prison offered by the National Park Service.

While the island indirectly generated income for Hollywood, the cost of maintaining a federal prison at Alcatraz continued to rise. The 336 cells rarely held more than 260 convicts at one time. As a federal prison, it housed in total only 1,547 inmates, although 1,576 numbers were issued: More than 30 inmates returned to

CASINO BY ACE ARCHITECTS

the Rock, and some were issued new identification numbers. By the early 1960s, the $10 a day it cost to board an inmate made it the most expensive prison in the federal system. To repair the crumbling walls, corroding pipes, and general disrepair, bring it up to seismic standards, and upgrade the security would cost the U.S. government more than $5 million. To order it closed was not a difficult decision, and in 1963 Attorney General Robert F. Kennedy did so.

But a new question arose: What to do with the island after its closure? The General Services Administration took over Alcatraz after the Department of Justice, but no one, it seemed, knew what to do with the empty island prison. The government began to solicit ideas. One group wanted to establish a memorial to the UN, which had its first organizational meeting in San Francisco in April 1945, but the State Department opposed the idea because they felt the site was too notorious. With no viable development, the General Services Administration deemed the land surplus and awaited developments.

The mayor of San Francisco at the time, Joseph Alioto, wasted no time in asking the public for ideas. (*Figures 64–66*) He was flooded with suggestions, from a gangster wax museum to a theme park, from an international center for the humanities

TOWER SCHEME ANNOUNCING THE WESTERN
GATEWAY TO THE U.S.A. SIMILAR IN SCALE TO
THE STATUE OF LIBERTY ON THE EAST COAST
· 1969 ·

to an animal and bird sanctuary. A casino was another proposal. The San Francisco Board of Supervisors then heard a plan from Lamar Hunt, son of Texas oil tycoon H. L. Hunt, to turn the island into an adult amusement park, akin to Las Vegas, with space travel as its theme. The supervisors gave tacit approval, but opposition soon materialized, partly directed at Hunt's right-wing politics. San Franciscans reacted strongly, forming an effective write-in campaign, and the project was stopped.

Finally, the General Services Administration accepted a proposal for a comprehensive park system that would incorporate the Presidio, the Headlands across the Golden Gate in Marin County, and Alcatraz. This plan would develop into the Golden Gate National Park Association, later changed to the Golden Gate National Parks Conservancy. The plan took effect just as the island was about to take on yet another identity: At the center of increasingly vocal American Indian civil rights protests, the island would become of the site of a nineteen-month occupation, beginning in November 1969.

CHAPTER 7

OCCUPATION

Alcatraz Is Not an Island

—PETER BLUE CLOUD, 1972

The title of Peter Blue Cloud's book of poetry symbolizes the transformation of Alcatraz Island into a place that linked the past with the present. As American Indians sought their civil rights, they took action to reclaim the island, but not before the last prisoner to leave Alcatraz offered a different view: "This place ain't never been no good for nobody," Frank Weatherman (AZ 1576) muttered in November 1963 as he stepped away from the island prison. The difference between these two views would define the fate of Alcatraz for the next generation.

One year after the government closure of the prison in 1963, the first of two brief attempts to "invade" the island occurred. In March of 1964, a group of forty Sioux with a lawyer occupied the island for a few hours. The unofficial warden, former associate warden Richard Willard, raced to the island and confronted the invaders and the attending press. "Trespassing, you are trespassing!" he shouted. On the advice of its lawyer, the group dispersed to their chartered tug, and within four hours, it was over.

Ironically, just three days before the Sioux occupation, a specially appointed presidential commission had quietly, if not secretly, met on the island to discuss a problem: No federal department could come up with any practical use for the worn-out prison.

At this time, while the government struggled to find a use for Alcatraz, American Indians had begun to assert their claim to civil rights, buoyed by the efforts of African Americans. The 1964 Civil Rights Act excluded American Indians, but by the end of the 1960s and into the '70s, the issue of equal rights was gaining momentum. Although American Indians indigenous to the area had been visiting Alcatraz since before its earliest discovery, the courts discredited the 1964 effort of the Sioux to claim the island.

THE MAJOR ISLAND OCCUPIERS ORIGINATED FROM THE ABOVE TRIBAL AREAS   1969-1971

America's "Devil's Island"— as Philip Grosser, a conscientious objector to the First World War imprisoned at Alcatraz, called it—sat uninhabited except for a series of former prison officials who were caretakers. But when the General Service Administration declared that the surplus island property could be offered to the city of San Francisco, a San Francisco American Indian group began to brainstorm.

Adam Fortunate Eagle, an activist and San Francisco American Indian leader and chair of the United Bay Area Council, contacted a San Francisco supervisor to offer to take over the island for cultural purposes. Following the burning of the San Francisco Indian Center in the Mission District in October 1969, Alcatraz as a new home made sense. American Indian groups in Oakland and San Francisco began to see the rationale in securing the island. These social activists, not militants, sought to recover land that once belonged to their ancestors. (*Figure 67*) Such action would also give rise and energy to the American Indian Movement (AIM) and the National Indian Youth Council.

Occupation Day was November 9, 1969, and the major media was alerted to the latest attempt to secure the island. Many Indians arrived in their traditional dress. Students from

GRAPHIC FOR ANNUALLY
HELD ALCATRAZ INDIAN
SOLIDARITY GATHERING

GRAPHIC FOR INDIANS
OF ALL TRIBES · 1970
DESIGNED BY DANA

UC Berkeley and San Francisco State joined the group, which had prepared a proclamation. The captain of a replica clipper ship gallantly took the party of seventy-five out to the island, but he did not want them to land, although several jumped off his boat and swam to shore. Except for the three that landed (removed by the coast guard), the group ended up circling the island and returning to Pier 39. The media photographed and reported the event, but no one ever expected a second attempt—on the same day. That's exactly what happened: That evening, fourteen Indians successfully jumped off a chartered fishing boat and scampered onto the water barge attached to the old loading dock of the island. A call to the caretaker, John Hart, found him incredulous: "What Indians? There aren't any more Indians!" he shouted into the phone to an inquiring but knowledgeable reporter.

The next day, an army of reporters and the coast guard descended on the island, which had fallen into disrepair since its closure in 1963: Vines grew about old concrete railings, while rusted iron reinforcing bars and shreds of oxidized bolts were everywhere. With the General Services Administration and the press on the island, Richard Oakes, titular leader of the fourteen, declared their victory and then surrender, after reading their proclamation, which began "We, the Native Americans, reclaim the land known as Alcatraz Island in the name of all American Indians by right of discovery." (*Figure 68*) National attention was now focused on the attempt and the realization

THE 'NO NAME BAR' IN SAUSALITO BECAME THE MEETING PLACE OF THE SAUSALITO - INDIAN NAVY

SYMBOLIC TEPEE ANNOUNCING
THE OCCUPATION OF ALCATRAZ

among American Indians that another, larger invasion must be undertaken.

Eleven days later, at 2 a.m. on November 20, 1969, a contingent calling themselves Indians of All Tribes began a nineteen-month occupation of the island with the hope of turning it into a university and cultural center. The help of the "Sausalito Indian Navy," three boats owned by a several sympathetic Californians, made the "reinvasion" possible. (*Figure 69*) By the time the "navy" had finished its job that night, ninety-two Indians, including two children, landed. The rookie watchman and caretaker Glenn Dodson was at first startled but then rather enjoyed the company of the "invaders." He did not alert the coast guard. At one point, he even got out his bagpipes to greet the last load of Indians who landed in the early dawn light. When the official caretaker, John Hart, returned, rather than contact authorities, he showed the invaders the location of the three working toilets.

Public reaction to the event was positive. No one at this stage condemned the action or suggested it was a criminal act or threat to the government. To take back a symbol of repression and punishment was inspired. And the action quickly took on a meaning beyond the symbolic: It became a rallying point for a reinvigorated American Indian movement across the United States. (*Figure 70*)

Yet, the reality of living on the island was quite challenging. Ideology was one thing, food another. Sustaining the occupation posed challenges, from food and water to safety. Washington was suddenly involved through both the General Services Administration and the White House. But the regional administrator of the GSA understood the delicacy of the situation and tried to delay any move by federal marshals to empty the island. He recognized the Indian claim to surplus federal property and knew that Alcatraz was certainly deserted. The media had by now also gotten the story, and suddenly the public was fascinated as boats of all shapes and sizes (including a sampan) began to appear at the edge of the formerly off-limits island. Curiosity about the once-secretive island mixed with public support for the invasion,

INDIAN POSTER 1970

INDIAN GRAPHIC 1970

essentially the first recapture of federal territory by American Indians in the twentieth century. (*Figure 71*)

Standoffs, compromises, and delays followed, as the occupation enlarged over the next nineteen months. The San Francisco Indian Center suddenly received money, food, blankets, and other items for the occupiers. On the island, LaNada Means and her two-year-old son settled in as she repainted signs that now read KEEP OFF. INDIAN PROPERTY. Other graffiti that claimed THIS LAND IS MY LAND, below the American eagle at the entrance to the Administration Building, or WARNING: KEEP OFF INDIAN PROPERTY, near the dock, formed a new visual dialogue with history, challenging the ownership of the island. (*Figures 72–75*) LaNada Means also set up an informal political council to balance Richard Oakes's focus on media and publicity. Means was the principal

Opposite: Figure 71
Below: Figure 72

PRISON SIGN WITH INDIAN
MODIFICATION   1969

"WARNING, KEEP OFF OF U.S.
INDIAN PROPERTY" 1969

figure in drafting a new document that had two key demands: that Interior Secretary Walter Hickel personally surrender the island to the band and that the government fund the construction of a cultural heritage and education center as reparation for previous thefts of Indian land. (*Figures 76–77 & 79*)

The coast guard didn't know what to do: The rule about keeping two hundred yards away was to prevent anyone from assisting escaping prisoners; they did not quite know what to do about those who wanted to stay. By the end of the second day, nearly 150 were on the island.

As the occupation continued, the "Sausalito Indian Navy" maintained supply runs and moved more Indians to the island, often at night. By December 1969, the Big Rock School opened for the twelve children then in residence. There was even a

daycare center and nursery. A clinic opened, visited frequently by mainland doctors.

A core group of fifty stayed on the island from the beginning, but visitors often came and went. Any tribal member who stayed a week or more earned a vote on the governing council. But at night, often fewer than fifty stayed. The absence of power and heat as the winter descended meant that staying on was an ordeal. Only the insulated Officers' Quarters or barracks provided some respite from the cold.

It later became clear that the American Indian Movement (*Figure 78*) had nothing to do with the Alcatraz occupation, although many thought they were behind the action. They did not even have any representatives in the Bay Area at the time; it was a local activist, Richard Oakes, who became the public face of the

GRAFFITI ADDED
BY THE INDIANS

MAIN CELL BLOCK ENTRY
WITH ALTERED SHIELD

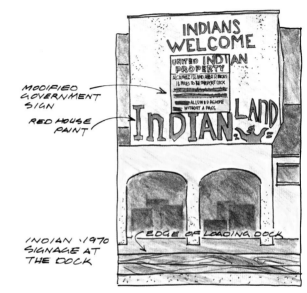

MODIFIED
GOVERNMENT
SIGN

RED HOUSE
PAINT

INDIAN 1970
SIGNAGE AT
THE DOCK

EDGE OF LOADING DOCK

INDIAN GRAFFITI INSIDE
THEIR OCCUPIED LIVING
QUARTERS   1970

INDIAN SIGNAGE AT
MAIN CELL BLOCK ENTRY
1969

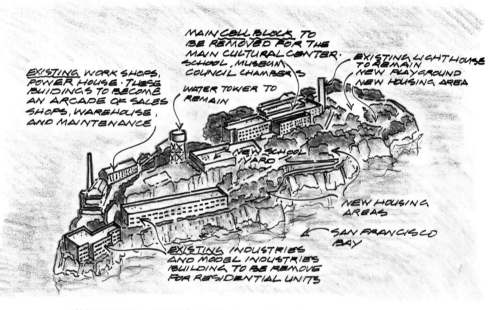

EXISTING, WORK SHOPS, POWER HOUSE. THESE BUILDINGS TO BECOME AN ARCADE OR SALES SHOPS, WAREHOUSE, AND MAINTENANCE.

MAIN CELL BLOCK TO BE REMOVED FOR THE MAIN CULTURAL CENTER. SCHOOL, MUSEUM COUNCIL CHAMBERS

WATER TOWER TO REMAIN

EXISTING LIGHTHOUSE TO REMAIN NEW PLAYGROUND NEW HOUSING AREA

NEW SCHOOL YARD

NEW HOUSING AREAS

SAN FRANCISCO BAY

EXISTING INDUSTRIES AND MODEL INDUSTRIES BUILDING TO BE REMOVE FOR RESIDENTIAL UNITS

EXISTING BUILDING AND SITE CONDITIONS ON ISLAND WITH PROPOSED CHANGES FOR AN INDIAN CENTER

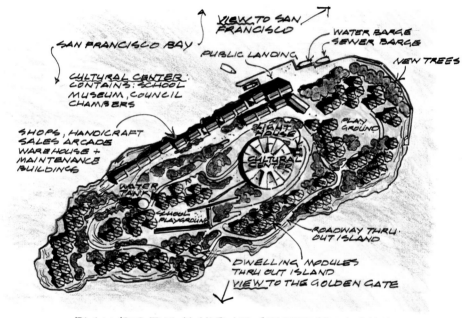

VIEW TO SAN FRANCISCO

SAN FRANCISCO BAY

PUBLIC LANDING

WATER BARGE SEWER BARGE

NEW TREES

CULTURAL CENTER: CONTAINS: SCHOOL MUSEUM, COUNCIL CHAMBERS

LIGHT HOUSE

PLAY GROUND

SHOPS, HANDICRAFT SALES ARCADE WAREHOUSE + MAINTENANCE BUILDINGS

CULTURAL CENTER

WATER TANK

SCHOOL PLAYGROUND

ROADWAY THRU OUT ISLAND

DWELLING MODULES THRU OUT ISLAND

VIEW TO THE GOLDEN GATE

PLAN FOR THE ALCATRAZ CENTER FOR INDIAN LIFE · DEVELOPED DURING THE OCCUPATION OF THE ISLAND BY NATIVE AMERICANS (1969-71) DESIGNED BY DONALD MACDONALD FOR INDIANS OF ALL TRIBES

occupation. The young man had formerly been the head of the small Native American Union at San Francisco State University and had played a prominent and unassailable

BADGE OF THE INDIAN MOVEMENT

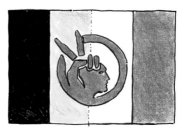

FLAG OF THE AMERICAN INDIAN MOVEMENT

Washington stalled, largely because they could not come up with a solution. The proposed formation of the Golden Gate National Recreation Area, which

role in both the earlier attempt at reclaiming the land and the present occupation. Gradually, a power struggle took place on the island, and then tragedy: the death of Oakes's stepdaughter, Yvonne, on January 3, 1970. Playing with other children, she fell through the railing of an apartment stairway bordering the concrete courtyard and tumbled three stories. A helicopter flew her to a San Francisco hospital where she died four days later. Could she have been pushed by Oakes's enemies? An inquiry found no evidence, but Oakes remained unconvinced. He gave up his leadership and withdrew from any involvement.

ran from Point Reyes in the north to the Presidio, excluded Alcatraz, which the American Indians had vowed would never be part of a national park scheme. But the White House, the FBI, and the Department of Justice were getting impatient. Meanwhile, the occupiers were gathering resources and making plans: They now had their own boat, a fishing/passenger vessel named *The Clearwater*, whose purchase was made possible by the band Creedence Clearwater Revival, and San Francisco architect Donald MacDonald was drawing up plans for an Indian university on the island, which would enroll three hundred students. Called

CULTURE CENTER
FOR SCHOOL, MUSEUM
COUNCIL CHAMBERS

SHOPS, HANDICRAFT SALES
ARCADE, WAREHOUSE AND
MAINTENCE BUILDINGS

MULTIPLE
STARS

ALCATRAZ INDIAN
FLAG
RED-WHITE-BLUE

SCHOOL YARD

LIGHT
HOUSE

DWELLING
UNITS SIMILAR
TO MODIFIED
WIGWAM
SHAPE

ROADWAY
AROUND ISLAND

SAN FRANCISCO
BAY

DESIGNED BY DONALD MACDONALD FOR
INDIANS OF ALL TRIBES

PARTIAL VIEW OF CULTURAL
CENTER FOR INDIAN LIFE

Thunderbird University, the estimated $6-million complex was to contain a large ceremonial roundhouse surrounded by ninety-six other circular buildings intended to be residences. LaNada Means and John Trudell held a news conference on the island unveiling the plans for the school. (*Figure 77*)

At a secret meeting with the occupation leaders in Tiburon, the government offered them part of Fort Mason on the San Francisco shoreline in return for giving up their claim to Alcatraz. They refused. The situation grew worse when drugs and violence began to play a role. A daily radio broadcast from the island on Berkeley's KPFA station helped inform the public of general order, although events became more politicized. Demands for money for the permanent American Indian university, requested by LaNada Means, became the next step, but at this stage it was only a wish.

Divisions and disputes soon occurred among the leaders as the government grew impatient and the Indians more inspired. Fear of infiltration by "agents" created a low-level paranoia on the island. Low-flying planes provided surveillance photos. The military and federal marshals even planned a secret counter-invasion—code name "Operation Parks." And in response to the rejection of the park proposal, the government cut supplies of water and power to the island. The lighthouse

THE COAST GUARD SHIP THAT EVACUATED THE OCCUPIERS OF ALCATRAZ   JUNE 11TH 1971

light was extinguished, and the coast guard put up new anchored buoys with their own beacons. The island went dark. And then, on the foggy night of June 1, 1971, fire broke out on the island, resulting in major damage. A strange yellow-orange glow emerged in the fog, visible to the mainland; when the coast guard sent a craft out to investigate, they discovered that the entire east side of the island was in flames. Centered at the top of the hill in the warden's home, the fire destroyed the Officers' Club and the lighthouse, symbol of the history and identity of the island.

After the fire, the *San Francisco Chronicle* quietly aided in the repair of the key lighthouse bulb. Initially wanting to supply a new power generator to ensure the continued operation of the lighthouse, the editor-in-chief of the paper, Scott Newhall, knew it would be impossible after the fire. But he secretly arranged for Tim Findley, a reporter who had befriended many on the island in the early days of the occupation, to go with the paper's chief electrician to replace the bulb. The lighthouse was relit on June 4, 1971, the *Chronicle* running a front-page story but not revealing their role in the event. Johnny Trudell, then the occupation spokesperson, explained that the relit light was "a symbol of the rekindled hope that someday the just claims and rightful dignity of the American Indians will be recognized."

The idealist phase of the early "invaders," many of them students, passed into a more difficult gang or street phase and then into a final phase of negotiations and resolution. The gutted shell of the warden's house visible from all over the San Francisco Bay stood as a reminder of the destruction and the occupation's apparent lack of leadership.

Conditions on the island continued to deteriorate. By the spring of 1971, basic services had been cut and supplies dwindled. Island population was transitory, and only a handful of Indians remained, with little to occupy their time. Meanwhile, FBI agents encouraged those with high balconies and porches in San Francisco to keep an eye on the island, and support for the occupation waned.

Efforts at settlement failed, and the government decided to act. Early on the morning of June 11, 1971, federal marshals and the coast guard, who had trained for weeks, embarked on a coast guard cutter. The invading party even had a disguise: Dressed in suits, they mimicked reporters if not U.S. marshals. They all were armed and told the occupiers that if they cooperated, no one would be handcuffed. It was a surprise and a success.

The fifteen Indians left on the island (six men, four women, and five children) went peacefully, traveling first to a military base at Yerba Buena Island and then to San Francisco. (*Figure 80*)

Organizer LaNada Means and spokesperson John Trudell were off the island seeking funds when the seizure took place. The following Monday, the press toured the island, but rather than finding it a symbol of American Indian achievement, they found a wreck. Windows had been broken, buildings ransacked, and wood dismantled to burn for heat. WHERE IS OUR CHIEF? read a hand-painted sign on a wall. After nineteen months and nine days, the nonviolent and unarmed occupation ended. But its symbolic and political importance lasted and accelerated a new engagement with Alcatraz and its future.

CHAPTER 8

GARDENS

They just whacked Mrs. Swisher. If she goes, that's it. We only have one of her. —GARDEN VOLUNTEER, ALCATRAZ, 2001

Mrs. Swisher was not a victim of Alcatraz vengeance but of pruning. A variety of fuchsia introduced to the island in 1942, the single pinkish flowers with white sepals and deep rosy corollas were distinctive. But by 2001, her future on the island was in jeopardy. Such was the fate of numerous flowers and plants accidentally or intentionally brought, dropped, or thrown at the sandstone summit of the mountain buried millennia earlier in the bay.

Post-occupation, Alcatraz was still in limbo. It took another year before Congress created the Golden Gate National Recreation Area in 1972—although not before the bulldozing of several island buildings, ostensibly to prevent another takeover. Only public criticism stopped the destruction (although the apartments were not saved). New legislation now included Alcatraz within the National Park Service, to be managed by rangers. And plans were in place to open Alcatraz to the public for the first time in its history.

The idea was to defuse the island's reputation as America's "Devil's Island," although the Park Service thought the public's interest would decline within four or five years. Alcatraz officially opened in October 1973, and in the first year, more visitors arrived than the population of its entire history. And the Park Service was wrong: Today, more than a 1.5 million visit the island each year, making it one of the most popular attractions in the country. The mystery of the prison, the only former or current federal prison that permits visitors, continues to fascinate.

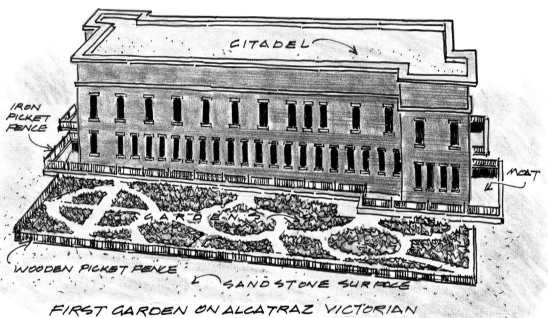

CITADEL

IRON PICKET FENCE

MOAT

GARDEN

WOODEN PICKET FENCE

SANDSTONE SURFACE

FIRST GARDEN ON ALCATRAZ VICTORIAN ERA 1869

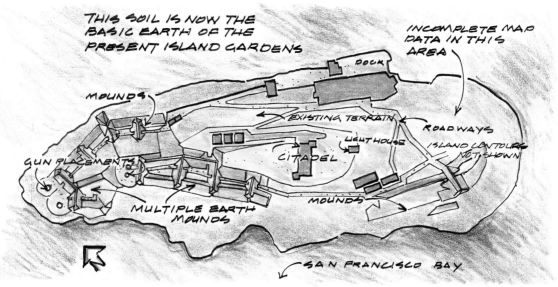

THIS SOIL IS NOW THE
BASIC EARTH OF THE
PRESENT ISLAND GARDENS

INCOMPLETE MAP
DATA IN THIS
AREA

MOUNDS

DOCK

EXISTING TERRAIN

ROADWAYS

LIGHTHOUSE

ISLAND CONTOURS
NOT SHOWN

CITADEL

GUN PLACEMENTS

MULTIPLE EARTH
MOUNDS

MOUNDS

SAN FRANCISCO BAY

1875 MAP OF ALCATRAZ ISLAND SHOWING
THE EARTH MOUNDS BUILT WITH SOIL MATERIAL
FROM THE ADJACENT ANGEL ISLAND

Natural life had also returned to the island. Sea life thrived in tidal pools, while monarch butterflies stopped every fall on their migration south. One of the most visible signs of the renewed

EARTH MOUNDS AT SOUTH END OF ISLAND CA. 1910

Alcatraz was its gardens, now internationally recognized. Grape hyacinths, artichokes, and scattered fruit trees populate the island, as do California poppies, gladiolus, and irises. The greenhouse, flowering terraces, rose gardens, and lawns have become important attractions on the island.

In his autobiography, *Long Walk to Freedom*, Nelson Mandela wrote of the value of a garden while he was imprisoned on Robben Island: "The sense of being the custodian of this small patch of earth offered a small taste of freedom." Prison gardens have, indeed, had a long history, beginning as the place for prisoners to grow their own food and often becoming part of rehabilitation.

At Alcatraz, gardening offered prisoners a modest control over their otherwise power-less situation, allowing them to domesticate an inhospitable environment and promote a semblance of normalcy. Gardens offered the dignity of work, opportunities for the expression of individual creativity, and a shared identity with nature. The beauty of the gardens offered solace and contrast to the cold, alien environment of Alcatraz. In a sense, the gardens became an anti-prison, a sub-versive response to imprisonment. In contrast to war and prison, gardens assert and celebrate the honor of life.

The gardens of Alcatraz predate the Civil War. The earliest grasses and flowers blossomed from seeds dropped or carried by the thousands of birds who were the island's first visitors. During the Civil War, when ships dropped off soil and seeds along with early prisoners, there was further germination. But

Alcatraz lacked the types of vegetation that would normally be found on an army post: native plant communities, areas for grazing, vegetable gardens, an orchard, or even ornamental vegetation. There was also almost no soil for gardening. At one point, as an economic move, Civil War soldiers cultivated a collection of vegetable gardens in a sheltered valley not far from Point Blunt known as "Alcatraz Gardens." The army found that growing produce there was cheaper than what was available at San Francisco's market prices. At the end of the Civil War, residents of Alcatraz began to excavate pockets in the rock and fill them with imported soil, allowing the introduction of garden areas and plants.

The first formal gardens on the island were ornamental, planted in 1869 or 1870 adjacent to the newly built Citadel. (*Figure 81*) Terraced gardens likely predated them. The soil that had been barged over from Angel Island to cushion cannonballs and protect battlements soon proved valuable for planting as well. (*Figure 82*) The Victorian garden had masonry paths, a picket fence, and ornamental stacks of cannonballs. Distinguished nineteenth-century photographer Eadweard Muybridge photographed officers' families relaxing there. Irrigating the areas were canvas hoses from underground cisterns. Another, smaller garden, sheltered from strong westerly winds, appeared just below the island's crest on the main access road.

Military logistics contributed to the remaking of the gardens. Gun emplacements on Alcatraz had to be redesigned after an attack on Fort Pulaski in Georgia in 1862 showed that the Third System of guns and defenses was out of date. (*Figure 83*) Beginning in 1869, the narrow gun terraces on Alcatraz were blasted to widen them, and the southern third of the island was leveled for the Parade Ground. It is estimated that by 1890, every yard of the island had either been cut away or infilled.

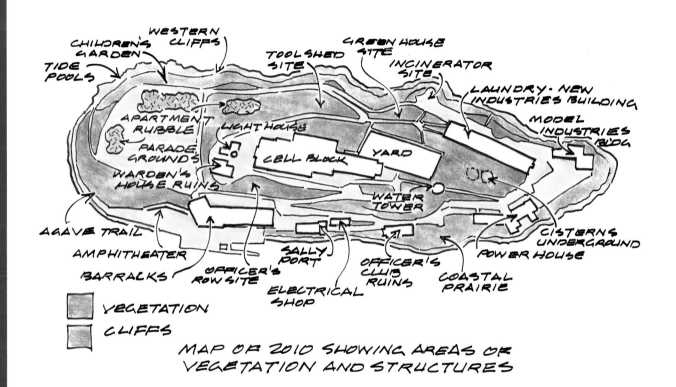

CHILDREN'S GARDEN
WESTERN CLIFFS
TIDE POOLS
TOOLSHED SITE
GREENHOUSE SITE
INCINERATOR SITE
LAUNDRY - NEW INDUSTRIES BUILDING
MODEL INDUSTRIES BLDG
APARTMENT RUBBLE
LIGHTHOUSE
PARADE GROUNDS
CELL BLOCK
YARD
WARDEN'S HOUSE RUINS
WATER TOWER
AGAVE TRAIL
AMPHITHEATER
BARRACKS
OFFICER'S ROW SITE
SALLY PORT
ELECTRICAL SHOP
OFFICER'S CLUB RUINS
COASTAL PRAIRIE
POWER HOUSE
CISTERNS UNDERGROUND

VEGETATION

CLIFFS

MAP OF 2010 SHOWING AREAS OF VEGETATION AND STRUCTURES

Opposite: Figure 84
Below: Figure 85

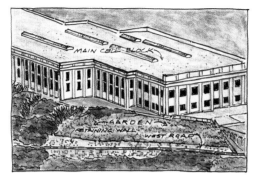

PERSPECTIVE SHOWING THE PLANTED
GARDEN OF THE "CELL HOUSE SLOPE"

The new defense plan required vast amounts of soil, and it came mostly from Angel Island—and with it came coyote brush, blue elderberry, and wild blackberry seeds, along with insects and small rodents. Additional new plants were introduced to control soil erosion: alfalfa, barley, and clover and later ivy, honeysuckle, and ice plant.

Replacing the garden in the lee of the Citadel in the 1880s was a row of three officers' cottages in a semi-Gothic style on the east side of the island, each with its own garden plot, windowboxes, and planters. The lighthouse keepers' quarters, at the end of Officers' Row, also had a garden.

Families tended separate plots with a focus on flowering plants rather than shrubbery. Color rather than geometry guided the plantings. The three large homes that were for the commandant and his officers contained small gardens with imported dirt, as well as poppies, geraniums, heliotropes, fuchsias, and calla lilies, according to a visiting lieutenant's report in 1895. By that time, flowerbeds and pots lined the switchback road to the summit of the island, originally blasted out in the 1850s.

The marine climate and wind required tough plants. They also had to tolerate frequent summer drought, since water was in short supply, although moisture from the fog helped. Most of the plants came from the Mediterranean, Mexico, South Africa, Australia, and South America and continue to flourish forty years after the prison closure. These included valerian, or heliotrope, a tall herb that originally grew on rocky sites around the Mediterranean; the mirror plant, a hedge species from the sea

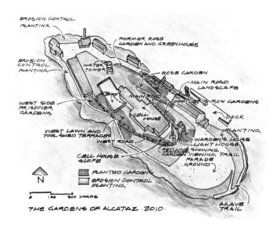

EROSION CONTROL PLANTING
FORMER ROSE GARDEN AND GREENHOUSES
EROSION CONTROL PLANTING
WATER TOWER
ROSE GARDEN
MAIN ROAD LANDSCAPE
WEST SIDE PRISONER GARDENS
MAIN ROAD
OFFICER'S ROW GARDENS
CELL HOUSE
DOCK
PLANTING
WEST LAWN AND TOOL SHED TERRACES
WEST ROAD
WARDEN'S HOUSE
LIGHTHOUSE
SEDUM SHOWING GARDEN VIEWING TRAIL PARADE GROUND
CELL HOUSE SLOPE
PLANTED GARDENS
EROSION CONTROL PLANTING
N
0   100   200 YARDS
THE GARDENS OF ALCATAZ · 2010 ·
AGAVE TRAIL

cliffs of New Zealand; and agave, a desert plant that thrives in moderate climates in western Mexico. Fuchsia, originally from the New World tropics, also did well on the island.

In 1923 and 1924, the California Spring Blossom and Wildflower Association began an aggressive island beautification project. Select inmates received training in gardening and pruning, and they planted three hundred donated trees, including eucalyptus, cypress, and pine. Despite shortages of water and proper maintenance, some gardens thrived under the management of the prisoners.

When the Bureau of Prisons took over in 1933, Fred Reichel, Warden Johnston's secretary, was so impressed by the army gardens that he began to maintain them himself. Reichel began with native California plants—the white-flowered bush puppy and the yellow-flowered flannel bush, no longer there—but he needed tough plants that could thrive despite neglect, such as the blue-flowered Pride of Madeira.

Reichel began with a single plant from a Los Angeles nurseryman; it still survives. Succulents also became important, notably aeonium, aloe, and sedum and the ubiquitous ice and century plants. Reichel later used salvage materials to build garden terraces, secured new plants in the old greenhouse, and lobbied for, and trained, inmate gardeners. He personally cared for the garden's fifty roses during his tenure (1934–1941). Every Sunday, he left cut flowers on the dock for island families.

'CALLA' NATIVE
TO SOUTH AFRICA

'NASTURTIUM'
NATIVE TO SOUTH
AMERICA

By the end of 1941, prisoner Elliott Michener became a full-time gardener for the area east of the fence dividing the slope. He spent nine years on the task, and it was he who discovered that fuchsias, originally from tropical Central and South America, would thrive all over the Rock. On the strip of hill beside the steps to the New Industries Building, Michener created a carpet of color with delphiniums, chrysanthemums, dahlias, and irises. He began by digging up the hardpan, fertilizing it with decomposing garbage, and then planting Iceland poppies, snapdragon, and stock. Another inmate, Dick Franseen, gardened on the other side of the island and gave Michener seeds and seed catalogs to study. Franseen had a greenhouse, as Michener later did.

During this period, gardens occupied the windward side of the island on the slopes below the cellhouse and by 1946 formed a luxuriant carpet of bushes, shrubs, and even fruit trees. Michener soon supplied flowers for the warden's house and helped Warden Swope's wife raise begonias in her small greenhouse until his release in 1950. After he'd served his sentence for counterfeiting, Michener made a living as a landscaper. In a letter, he wrote, "If we are all our own jailers, and prisoner of our traits, then I am grateful for my introduction to the spade and trowel, the seed and the spray can."

Interestingly, the type of plant reflects the times. In the Victoria era, gardens favored showy, exotic plants. Later, low-growing ice plant and honeysuckle were introduced to prevent

'SPURIA IRIS'
NATIVE TO
EUROPE

ROSA 'DORTHY PERKINS'
NATIVE TO EAST ASIA

ARTICHOKE
NATIVE OF THE
MEDITERRANEAN
BASIN

MONTBRETIA
NATIVE OF SOUTH
AFRICA

soil erosion, and windbreaks such as cypress and eucalyptus were planted. Native plants such as poppies and lupine, as well as nasturtiums and trees, became a part of the beautification project. Individual gardeners had special interests, too: for Freddie Reichel, it was rare plants; for officers and staff, it was roses and fuchsias; inmate gardeners favored bulbs and brightly flowering plants. New botanical variations were the result of these individual gardening choices.

There were also seaside plants tolerant of salty winds, fog, and rocky or shallow soils, such as Monterey cypress and the Australian tea tree, shrubs like the Sydney golden wattle and the Pride of Madeira, and succulents like aeonium, century plant, torch plant, and Hottentot fig. Annuals included the red valerian and California poppy. Fruit trees require care and warm climate, but several have survived on the island: In the greenhouse garden area below the recreation yard are an apple, peach, walnut, and several fig trees. Other plants have invaded accidentally, transferred from the clothing, shoes, or tools brought by visitors. Pampas grass, false garlic, Bermuda buttercup, and blackberry are several examples. German ivy is another colonizer, as is the poisonous nightshade.

Starting in 2003, the National Park Service, the Golden Gate National Parks Conservancy, and the Garden Conservancy created the Alcatraz Historic Gardens Project to restore the gardens planted in the island's military and prison eras, using

PELARGONIUM 'PRINCE
BISMARCK'
NATIVE TO SOUTH AFRICA

'RED HOT POKER'
NATIVE TO
SOUTH AFRICA

Opposite: Figure 90
Below: Figure 91

PRIDE OF MADEIRA
NATIVE OF NORTH AFRICA

CHASMANTHE
FLORIBUNDA
NATIVE OF SOUTH
AFRICA

LILY OF THE NILE
NATIVE OF SOUTH
AFRICA

DROSANTHEMUM
FLORIBUNDA
NATIVE OF SOUTH
AFRICA

Opposite: Figure 92
Next Page: Figure 93

historical photographs as reference. Garden restoration, led by the Garden Club of San Francisco, is currently focusing on the main entry road up from the sally port, Officers' Row, the warden's house and the cellblock slopes, and the west-side gardens. (*Figures 85–86*) The once-soilless environment of Alcatraz now supports more than 145 plant species. Today, fuchsia hangs down the retaining walls along the access road; valerian runs wild in the shell of the warden's house; and elderberry, coyote brush, privet, and mirror plant grow on the southwestern slope below the cellblock. Even geraniums and Asian roses bloom along with fig trees and apple trees in the remains of a greenhouse. (*Figure 84*)

'HOMERIA COLLINA'
NATIVE TO SOUTH
AFRICA

FUCHSIA 'ROSE OF
CASTILE'
NATIVE TO SOUTH
AMERICA

BELOW IS A SAMPLE LIST OF PLANTS CURRENTLY THRIVING ON THE ISLAND, WHICH BECAME A NATIONAL HISTORIC LANDMARK IN 1986: (*Figures 87–93*)

AGAVE
ARTICHOKE
BEAR'S-BREECH
CALIFORNIA BLACKBERRY
CALIFORNIA POPPY
CALLA LILY
CAPE TULIP
COBRA LILY
EUCALYPTUS
FIRECRACKER FUCHSIA
GERANIUM
HONEYSUCKLE
LILY OF THE NILE
MONTBRETIA
MONTEREY CYPRESS

NASTURTIUM
PINK ICE PLANT
PRIDE OF MADEIRA (SHRUB)
PRINCE BISMARCK PELARGONIUM
RED VALERIAN
ROSE (ROSE DE CASTILE, MEMORIAL ROSE,
    ROSA DOROTHY PERKINS)
SPURIA IRIS
TORCH LILY OR RED HOT POKER
TORCH PLANT

CHAPTER 9

BIRDS OF ALCATRAZ

For not even yet is our knowledge
of the birds of California perfected.
—WILLIAM LEON DAWSON, "A PERSONAL SUPPLEMENT TO THE DISTRIBUTIONAL
LIST OF THE BIRDS OF CALIFORNIA," 1916

The above response to Joseph Grinnell's magisterial work *A Distributional List of the Birds of California* (1915)—the first major study of birds in the west—is especially apt for Alcatraz. From their earliest sighting, birds have defined the island: Pelicans, of course, lent their name to the outcropping. Forty-niners arriving for the California gold rush called Alcatraz "Bird Island" or "White Island" because of its profusion of birds, and prisoner Nathan Williams, AZ 1103, said the incessant noise of birds drowned out the sound of other inmates and even the foghorn: "There was a lot to despise about the place. But I really hated those damn birds," he said. (*Figure 94*)

Though bare of any vegetation and lacking fresh water, Alcatraz likely supported one of the major seabird colonies in central California before human intervention. Its location in the middle of the bay perhaps offered protection from predators and became a natural habitat. At the time Ayala, the Spanish naval officer, first saw the islands we now call Alcatraz and Yerba Buena, they were covered by pelicans. Early Indian visitors traveled in their reed canoes to the island to retrieve seabird eggs. But birdlife on the island since then has been rocky at best. In Grinnell's detailed listing, Alcatraz does not appear as a nesting center. As the island was reshaped as a fortress, and inhabitants—whether soldiers or inmates—grew, large colonies of birds disappeared. Nesting was simply not viable, "Island of Pelicans" or not.

Surprisingly, humans may have encouraged a bird population even as they took over their environment. The transported soil from Angel Island, which contained plants and microorganisms,

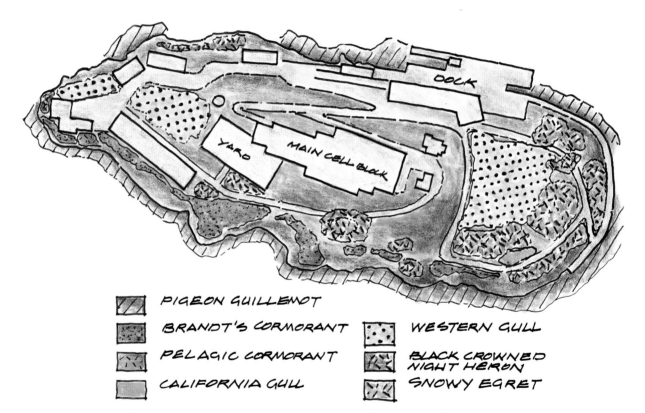

DOCK

YARD   MAIN CELL BLOCK

| | PIGEON GUILLEMOT
| | BRANDT'S CORMORANT
| | PELAGIC CORMORANT
| | CALIFORNIA GULL

| | WESTERN GULL
| | BLACK CROWNED NIGHT HERON
| | SNOWY EGRET

BIRD NESTING AREAS ON ALCATRAZ ISLAND

WESTERN GULL
HABITAT: COASTAL
ISLANDS NEAR WATER

NEST: IN SMALL
COLONIES · ON THE
GROUND · 3 EGGS
PER NEST

and the ornamental plants, shrubs, and trees planted during the military fort and federal prison years, offered birds vegetation, now a major source of sustenance. Since the close of the federal prison in 1963, many birds have found the uninhabited island a welcoming, protective sanctuary, and areas set aside as protective habitat in the 1990s have allowed vegetation to grow wild, enticing birds to the island.

Biologists have noted that, despite constant sea traffic, visitors, and low-flying aircraft, western gulls began to recolonize the island circa 1973 and now form the largest colony in the Bay Area. They are also Alcatraz's main species, with 510 nests located as early as 1998. Black-crowned night herons returned in 1975, and the bay's only colonies of pigeon guillemots, pelagic cormorants, and Brandt's cormorants began to appear in 1982, 1986, and 1991, respectively. Snowy egrets came in 1997, as did a single pair of black oyster catchers. (*Figures 95–101*) By 1999, there were more than 248 Brandt's cormorant and approximately 19 pelagic cormorant nests on the western cliffs. Also counted were the nests of black-crowned night herons (240), pigeon guillemots (21), snowy egrets (15), and a single black oyster catcher nest. The southern and southwestern shorelines, consisting of relatively inaccessible twenty-meter cliffs, are where most seabirds nest.

The resurgence of birds on Alcatraz confirms the island's regeneration. In the first decade or so of the new millennium, more than 108 species, including the endangered brown pelican and peregrine falcon, have settled or stopped on the twenty-two-acre island. A 2006 study on the breeding of seabirds on Alcatraz attributed the repopulation of birds on the island to the accessibility of fish in the

BLACK·CROWNED NIGHT·
HERON
HABITAT: SALT WATER AREAS
IN SHRUBS·THICKETS·REEDS

NEST: LOCATED WITH HERONS
MADE OF STICKS·REEDS
WITH FINE LINING·3
EGGS PER NEST.

PIGEON GUILLEMOT
HABITAT: PERIMETERS
OF ROCKBOUND ISLANDS

NEST LOCATED AMONGST
LOOSE ROCKS AND BOULDERS
ABOVE THE HIGH TIDE LINE
USALLY 2 EGGS PER NEST

BROWN
SPOTS

THE FOLLOWING IS A SAMPLE LIST OF THE MAJOR BIRDS CURRENTLY NESTING ON THE ISLAND:

BARN SWALLOW

BLACK PHOEBE

BLACK-CROWNED NIGHT HERON

BRANDT'S CORMORANT

CALIFORNIA GULL

COMMON RAVEN

EUROPEAN STARLING

HOUSE FINCH

MALLARD

MOURNING DOVE

PELAGIC CORMORANT

PIGEON GUILLEMOT

ROCK DOVE

SNOWY EGRET

SONG SWALLOW

WESTERN GULL

NONBREEDING BIRDS THAT APPEAR FREQUENTLY ON ALCATRAZ:

AMERICAN KESTREL

BELTED KINGFISHER

BLACK TURNSTONE

BROWN PELICAN

CALIFORNIA TOWHEE

COMMON MURRE

DOUBLE-CRESTED CORMORANT

HERMIT THRUSH

NORTHERN FLICKER

RED-TAILED HAWK

SANDERLING

SURF SCOTER

SURFBIRD

WANDERING TATTLER

WESTERN GREBE

NEST: ON THE
GROUND IN COLONIES.
3 EGGS PER NEST

CALIFORNIA GULL
HABITAT: COASTAL ISLANDS
NEAR WATER

PELAGIC CORMORANT
HABITAT: CLIFFS AND
ROCKY SHORES IN TIDAL
RIPS AND SURF

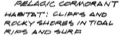

NEST: ON NARROW
LEDGE OF CLIFFS
IN COLONIES. 4
EGGS PER NEST

bay combined with seasonal protection of nesting habitats. The study also noted that breeding and roosting birds on Alcatraz were afforded legal protection as early as 1918 under the Migratory Bird Treaty Act. In order to ensure continued nesting and population growth, national park biologists barricade the north and south ends of Alcatraz for six months of the year, allowing the birds a quiet environment to breed—despite the average 4,900 visitors a day.

Among the many species documented on Alcatraz, some of the smaller breeds include Anna's hummingbirds, mallards, song sparrows, and common ravens. Nonbreeding species that appear frequently include the western grebe, the surf scoter, American kestrel, wandering tattler, Heermann's gull, belted kingfisher, northern flicker, and hermit thrush.

Under existing development and park management, almost 75 percent of the island is available to wildlife. But one of the challenges is to sustain the influx of visitors, while minimizing their impact on wildlife and the environment. Efforts to maintain the ecological balance is another concern, and closing parts of the island has actually created new wildlife habitats. The black-crowned night heron is known to nest in only twelve colonies in the Bay Area, so care must be taken for their presence on Alcatraz to be preserved. On the island, they nest principally in mirror bushes, fig trees,

BRANDT'S CORMORANT
HABITAT: COASTAL ISLANDS
NEAR A RELIABLE FOOD SUPPLY

NEST: IN COLONIES.
CLOSED - GROUPED.
GROUND NESTS ON
ROCKY CLIFFS. 4 EGGS
PER NEST

blackberry vines, and other trees and shrubs (but even rubble appeals to them: one of the black-crowned night heron nests sits in the middle of twisted metal and cement).

SNOWY EGRET
HABITAT: SALT WATER AREAS.
IN SHRUBS · THICKETS · REEDS

NEST: LOCATED WITH HERONS
MADE OF REEDS AND
RUSHES 4 EGGS PER
NEST

Human disturbance is the greatest threat to the black-crowned night heron and the western gulls, possibly the earliest inhabitants of the island. There are more than twenty-seven western gull nesting locations on the island, including the cistern, Agave Trail (where twenty-nine nests have been recorded), and the Parade Ground (where 20 percent of the gulls nest). Other birds like the pigeon guillemot prefer to nest on cliffs on the western and southern side of the island, mostly in holes dug in the mortar of the old brickworks or on the cliffs. Brandt's cormorants, by contrast, prefer to roost along the southwestern cliffs.

Other nesting sites include the northwestern cliffs below the Model Industries Building for the pelagic cormorant and the open trails for the white-crowned sparrow. The western cliffs are the most populated area, however, with pigeon guillemots, Brandt's cormorants, and pelagic cormorants. Also present are black-crowned night herons, western gulls, and, in the summer and fall, Heermann's gulls. The renewal of the bird population is one of the most manifest signs of the vital ecological role of Alcatraz, which will continue to grow.

Curiously, Robert Stroud, popularly known as the "Birdman of Alcatraz," never had birds on the island. He had canaries at Leavenworth Penitentiary and was actually known as the "Bird Doctor of Leavenworth." The real birdmen of the Rock are the biologists and national park rangers.

CHAPTER 10

ALCATRAZ TODAY & TOMORROW

If you San Franciscans had any true civic pride, you'd blow the place out of the water instead of advertising it. What an eyesore. —BURT LANCASTER AS ROBERT STROUD IN *BIRDMAN OF ALCATRAZ*

Ever since the American Indian Occupation, plans for Alcatraz have been presented, debated, rejected, and embraced. The National Park Service, under pressure to revitalize the space, and working with the Golden Gate National Recreation Area group, needed to work out a management scheme. By 1977, there were three options: clean up the rubble and leave historic buildings intact, offering guided tours; remove all but key historic structures and landscape the remaining open space; or stabilize historic structures and offer self-guided tours and other educational programs. The first option was chosen. But by the late '70s, growth in demand to visit the island required a reevaluation of policies. Additionally, harsh weather and limited services created low morale among the guides, overwhelmed by the large numbers of visitors. The third propsal, to reinforce the buildings and feature self-guided tours, then became policy. By 1980, according to the General Master Plan, historic preservation became the key goal, although the National Park Service also sought a proper landscaped setting in which the prison and military structures would stand in stark contrast. But the island had to learn to both handle the many visitors and be true to its principle of preservation.

By 1985, a new policy of self-guided tours was in place, and visitors could explore the island on their own, although ranger tours were still available. One feature of the guided tour was that at the end, the ranger would ask for silence and then clang shut a cell door. The sound reverberated throughout the crumbling halls of the cellhouse. The headset tour allowing for independent exploration included comments by former inmates Jim Quillen and Whitey Thompson.

The challenge was to convert Alcatraz from a prison to a park. Landscape architect Larry Halprin's 1988 report "Alcatraz: The Future," proposed a series of concepts for the island, creating an "open island," with shoreline walks, overlooks, and picnic areas. He also suggested restoring the Parade Ground and other public areas then bordered by rubble. (*Figure 102*) At the time he began his study in late November 1986, 80 percent of the island was closed to the public. Halprin's plan was to change that,

DEMOLISHED BUILDINGS NOW PILES OF RUBBLE ON THE PARADE GROUNDS

making the island look more like a nature preserve than a historic prison. To do this, he wanted to maximize public access to the physical spaces, stories, and even moods of Alcatraz. He wanted to change the experience of visitors from merely a tour of a former prison into an experience of a diverse and changing habitat. Among his suggestions was a perimeter walkway circling the island as close as possible to the water. Another was transforming the north plaza into a large sheltered open space, allowing it to become a viewing area of the Golden Gate Bridge, the Marin Headlands, and the Presidio. He even suggested the re-creation of a ten-inch Columbiad cannon and stacked cannonballs. The Parade Ground itself should reflect topographical changes with mounds

VIEW OF ALCATRAZ LOOKING NORTHEAST
2010

surrounded by low stone walls breaking the wind while providing seating. He recommended no changes to the cellblock, only expanded visitor programs. He also suggested improved night lighting to silhouette the island and make it the visible nighttime focus of the bay.

Design guidelines were especially clear, beginning with color. Halprin and his team suggested maintaining the monochromatic hues that already existed. The island's color comes via its plants. The appropriate shades for any renovation or new buildings should be shades of gray, white, and brown. Building materials should also reflect what already exists there, avoiding any form of plastic, shiny metal finishes, or bright polychromatic colors. Lighting should be discrete, limited to a garland of lights around the proposed perimeter walkway and uplighting of the historic lighthouse. Essentially, design for Alcatraz should be in keeping with what is already there, rejecting contemporary stylings or phony Victorian elements.

Halprin also suggested some new uses for the island: In addition to the prison tour, he suggested having certain national holiday observances, historical events, or gatherings of certain interest groups such as environmentalists, historians, or ethnobotanists. Nature walks, picnics, or even musical performances could also occur. Long-term considerations included turning a renovated Model Industries Building into a seminar and conference center, while the New Industries Building could have an architectural winter garden open from floor to ceiling with a café court at the bottom. He even thought that Building 64 at the dock might be renewed so that limited overnight guests could stay in a combined inn and hostel. His goal was to both maintain the architectural integrity of the island and allow its natural beauty to be exhibited.

ARMY FORTRESS AND PRISON 1859-1933

FEDERAL PRISON 1934-1963
INDIAN OCCUPATION 1969-1971

PATCH WITH SYMBOLIC REPRESENTATION OF THE HISTORY OF THE ISLAND
FORTRESS → PRISON → OCCUPATION → NATIONAL PARK

in the 1990s. The idea was partly to pay less attention to the prison and more to other features of the island. A new environmental assessment was released in 1993, marking the commitment of the park to integrate natural and cultural

The Golden Gate National Park Association submitted Halprin's plan to the National Park Service, supplementing the General Management Plan and an Interpretative Prospectus. To no one's surprise, the Audubon Society objected to the over-development of Alcatraz, and the National Park Service enacted only the Agave Trail from Halprin's imaginative plan.

The National Park Service then initiated a comprehensive program for the island, whose role as a bird refuge was growing

resources, the preservation of which became the overriding goal of the National Park Service and the public. The 1993 plan also balanced use, history, and nature on the island, confirming the principle of an "open island." Birds received equal standing with historic resources. The sales of gifts and souvenirs on the island facilitated the growth of the Golden Gate National Park Association. Revenue to the organization allowed for its own expansion and support of new island initiatives. And access to the island could always be controlled, particularly during stabilization and reconstruction projects, since visitors could get there only by boat. The new belief was that increased use and better protection of habitat were not mutually exclusive. Historic preservation and natural protection could, and do, coincide.

As birds continue to populate the island and the dominant westerlies carve the shape of the rock, (*Figure 103*) the rubble from older buildings reminds one of the rich heritage that survives on the island. Despite its long transformation from uninhabited island to fortress, prison, occupied land, national park, bird sanctuary, and botanical garden, Alcatraz's past lives in the present. It is a dynamic monument to a varied history that records the intersection of geography, weather, and culture—exposed for everyone to see.

Impressions of Alcatraz are as varied as those who visit the site. One visitor in the late '80s thought the sally port one of the most powerful spaces: "The play of light and shadow, the rifle slits, the sense of passage through a major portal all convey the feeling of going into the real Alcatraz. From the other side, however, it doesn't feel that secure." "The roadway switchbacks up to the cellhouse are like walking through the history of the island," commented another, illustrating the idea of the island's adaptability: Army barracks became a prison, a military chapel became the officers' rifle range, and cypress trees planted to beautify the space have now become home to the black-crowned night heron. These and thousands of other reactions mark the symbolism and mystery of Alcatraz—a place of exploration, education, creativity, reflection, and renewal—while confirming the island as its own sea of change. (*Figure 104*)

APPENDIX 1
ALCATRAZ IN THE MOVIES

To date, there have been thirty-three movies made about Alcatraz, ranging from *Alcatraz Island* (1937) to *Half Past Dead* (2002) and *Curse of Alcatraz* (2007). Directors have included John Frankenheimer, John Boorman, Otto Preminger, Paul Krasny, Philip Marcus, Don Siegel, and Michael Bay. In order of popularity, here are the seven top movies about the Rock.

BIRDMAN OF ALCATRAZ (*United Artists, 1962*)

Burt Lancaster plays convicted murderer Robert Stroud (1890–1963)—a.k.a. "The Birdman"—who resided at Alcatraz from 1942 to 1959. Filmed primarily at United Artists Studios, *Birdman of Alcatraz* also utilized exterior shots of the actual island prison in San Francisco Bay. The film earned four Oscar nominations: Best Actor (Lancaster), Best Supporting Actor (Telly Savalas), Best Supporting Actress (Thelma Ritter), and Best Cinematography (Burnett Guffey).

ESCAPE FROM ALCATRAZ (*Paramount, 1979*)

Clint Eastwood is Frank Morris, who, with the Anglin brothers, John and Clarence (played by Fred Ward and Jack Thibeau), bust out of Alcatraz on June 11, 1962. Patrick McGoohan plays the warden, who tells budding accordion player Morris: "That's one of the benefits of Alcatraz . . . lots of time to practice." Producer/director Don Segal filmed *Escape from Alcatraz* on the Rock. The production company had to lay fifteen miles of cable from the mainland in order to provide the former island prison with electricity.

THE ROCK (*Buena Vista, 1996*)

Brigadier General Frank Hummel (Ed Harris) and his renegade marines take over Alcatraz, threatening to kill their tourist hostages and level San Francisco with stolen rockets armed with chemical weapons. When a covert navy seal team is ambushed and killed, ex-Alcatraz con John Patrick Mason (Sean Connery) and FBI biochemist Dr. Stanley Goodspeed (Nicolas Cage) slip into the island fortress. "The Rock? When did they make it a tourist attraction?" Connery asks at one point in the film.

SEVEN MILES FROM ALCATRAZ (*RKO, 1942*)
Convict Champ Larkin (James Craig) and his pal Jimbo (Frank Jenks) take unofficial leave of Alcatraz, winding up at a lighthouse in San Francisco Bay. Here they encounter the lighthouse owner (George Cleveland) and his daughter (Bonita Granville), along with a nest of Nazi spies.

EXPERIMENT ALCATRAZ (*RKO, 1950*)
Alcatraz physician Dr. Ross Williams (John Howard) is busy on the Rock, using volunteer convicts for his medical experiments into blood diseases. The film is out of the Atomic/Red Scare era, with a radioactive potion becoming the pivot of the plot.

ALCATRAZ ISLAND (*Warner Bros., 1937*)
Racketeer "Gat" Brady (John Litel) winds up in Alcatraz on an income tax rap—the same charge that landed Al Capone in federal prison. Inside, Brady is framed for the murder of another convict. "It's just the same in here as being in your grave," Tough Tony Burke (George E. Stone) says of Alcatraz, "only you miss the fun of being dead."

MURDER IN THE FIRST (*Warner Bros., 1995*)
Kevin Bacon plays Henri Young, a petty thief who is sent to Alcatraz in 1938. Following an unsuccessful escape attempt, Young is placed in solitary confinement for three years. Emerging from his hellish ordeal, Young later faces a murder charge, where he is defended by novice public defender James Stamphill (Christian Slater).

OTHER NOTABLE ALCATRAZ FILMS:
King of Alcatraz (Paramount, 1938)
Train to Alcatraz (Republic, 1948)
Al Capone (Allied Artists, 1959)
Alcatraz Express (TV; Desilu, 1960)
Curse of Alcatraz (Grindstone, 2007)

Famous inmates
and their time
spent at the Rock:

AL CAPONE *1934–1939*

One of America's most popular gangsters, he was publically
known as Al "Scarface" Capone. A success at bootlegging,
casinos, and speakeasies and the mastermind of the infamous Saint Valentine's Day Massacre in Chicago in February
1929, he was jailed for tax evasion.

ALBERT BATES *1934–1948*

An associate of Kelly's, Bates helped him in the 1933 kidnap-
ping of an Oklahoma oil baron. He died at Alcatraz.

GEORGE "MACHINE GUN" KELLY *1934–1951*

For a time, Kelly was Public Enemy Number One. He transferred to Alcatraz after telling reporters he would break out
of Leavenworth.

HARMON WALEY *1935–1957*

Waley spent twenty-two years at the Rock, the longest continu-
ous period of incarceration on the island.

ALVIN "CREEPY" KARPIS *1936–1962*

Karpis spent a total of twenty-five years at Alcatraz, but his time
was broken up by a transfer to, and return from, Leavenworth.

FLOYD HAMILTON *1940–1952*

Hamilton was a bank robber and former member of the
Bonnie and Clyde Gang. He participated in an attempted
escape on April 14, 1943.

ROBERT STROUD *1942–1959*

The "Birdman of Alcatraz" ironically did not have any birds on
the island. He kept and studied birds at Leavenworth Prison in
Kansas before he arrived at the Rock.

MORTON SOBELL *1952–1957*

The most famous political prisoner at Alcatraz, he stood trial in
1951 with Julius and Ethel Rosenberg for espionage and treason
for stealing atomic secrets and passing them to the Russians.

Wardens at U.S. Penitentiary, Alcatraz:

JAMES A. JOHNSTON *1934–1948*

Johnston was a lawyer, banker, civic leader, and former warden
of Folsom Prison and San Quentin.

EDWIN B. SWOPE *1948–1955*

PAUL J. MADIGAN *1955–1961*

OLIN G. BLACKWELL *1961–1963*

Blackwell presided over Alcatraz's closing. Only twenty-seven
prisoners were left when they were led in handcuffs, leg
irons, and waist chains down Broadway, single file, out the
door, and onto waiting transportation on March 21, 1963.

APPENDIX 3
ESCAPE
ATTEMPTS

You've got to admit, it's a pretty piece of masonry, that Alcatraz, but it never was a choice spot for a vacation.

—CHAMP LARKIN, *SEVEN MILES FROM ALCATRAZ*, 1942

JOSEPH BOWERS *April 27, 1936*
Shot during attempt and fell to his death.

THEODORE COLE, RALPH ROE *December 16, 1937*
Believed to have drowned, but bodies never found.

RUFUS FRANKLIN, THOMAS LIMMERICK, JAMES LUCAS *April 23, 1938*
Attacked officers with a hammer. Limmerick died of gunshot wounds; Franklin and Lucas received life sentences.

ARTHUR "DOC" BARKER, WILLIAM MARTIN, RUFUS MCCAIN, DALE STAMPHILL, HENRI YOUNG *January 13, 1939*
Barker died on the way back to prison; the remainder stood trial for their escape attempt.

LLOYD BARKDOLL, JOSEPH P. CRETZER, ARNOLD T. KYLE, SAM SHOCKLEY *May 21, 1941*
All four surrendered before reaching the water.

JOHN R. BAYLESS *September 15, 1941*

Attempted escape from the garbage detail. Captured before reaching the water.

JAMES BOARMAN, HAROLD BREST, FLOYD HAMILTON, FRED HUNTER *April 14, 1943*

Boarman drowned; the others were captured.

TED WALTERS *August 7, 1943*

Captured before he made it to the water.

CLARENCE CARNES, BERNARD PAUL COY, JOE CRETZER, MARVIN F. HUBBARD, MIRAN THOMPSON, SAM SHOCKLEY *May 2, 1946*

Referred to as the 1946 riot. Coy, Cretzer, and Hubbard found dead in a utility corridor after military and police assault. Shockley and Thompson died in December in the gas chamber at San Quentin. Carnes given a second life sentence.

JOHN GILES *July 31, 1949*

Escaped to Angel Island in disguise of army sergeant. Captured on arrival at Angel Island.

FLOYD P. WILSON *July 23, 1956*

Disappeared from dock crew but captured on island before entering the water.

AARON BURGETT, CLYDE JOHNSON *September 29, 1958*

Overpowered a guard while on garbage detail. Burgett drowned. Johnson captured in the water and returned.

CLARENCE ANGLIN, JOHN W. ANGLIN, FRANK LEE MORRIS, ALLEN WEST *June 11, 1962*

Escape through the roof after leaving papier-mâché heads of themselves in their bunks. Never found. Plot of the movie *Escape from Alcatraz.*

JOHN PAUL SCOTT, DARL LEE PARKER *December 14, 1962*

Parker found on a rock near the island; Scott found near death at Fort Point.

RESOURCES & REFERENCES

Eagle, Adam Fortunate, in collaboration with Tim Findley. *Heart of the Rock: The Indian Invasion of Alcatraz.* Norman, OK: Oklahoma Univ. Press, 2002. A personal account of the American Indian Occupation.

The Gardens of Alcatraz. "History of Gardening on the Island." www.alcatrazgardens.org/history.php. A web site for the Gardens of Alcatraz.

Hart, John, et al. *Gardens of Alcatraz.* San Francisco: Golden Gate National Park Association, 1996.

Helphand, Kenneth I. *Defiant Gardens: Making Gardens in Wartime.* San Antonio: Trinity Univ. Press, 2006. The importance and role of gardens in desperate situations.

Ison, Tara. *A Child Out of Alcatraz.* Boston: Faber and Faber, 1997. A novel about growing up on Alcatraz with the history of the prison as backdrop.

Johnson, Troy R. *The Occupation of Alcatraz Island: Indian Self-Determination and the Rise of Indian Activism.* Urbana: Univ. of Illinois Press, 1996. A detailed historical study of the occupation set in the social context of the '60s and '70s.

Lutsko, Ron, and Robyn Menigoz. "The Historical Gardens of Alcatraz Island. Research for the Golden Gate National Park Association," 1992. Available at the Golden Gate National Recreation Area Headquarters, Fort Mason, San Francisco.

Martini, John Arturo. *Fortress Alcatraz: Guardian of the Golden Gate.* 1990; Berkeley: Ten Speed Press, 2004. A useful and well-illustrated account of the military history of Alcatraz with a glimpse at its prison years up through the 1980s.

National Park Service. "Alcatraz Island." www.nps.gov/alcatraz. An electronic tour of Alcatraz including video clips and interviews with former inmates and guards.

Quillen, James. *Alcatraz from Inside: The Hard Years 1942–1952.* San Francisco: Golden Gate National Park Association, 1991.

Saenz, Benjamin, et al. "An Urban Success Story: Breeding Seabirds on Alcatraz Island, California, 1990–2002," *Marine Ornithology* 34 (2006): 43–49.

Thompson, Erwin. *The Rock: A History of Alcatraz Island 1847–1972.* Denver: National Park Service, 1979. A landmark historical study completed for the National Park Service in 1974.

Ward, David, with Gene Kassebaum. *Alcatraz: The Gangster Years.* Berkeley: Univ. of California Press, 2009. A comprehensive survey of the prison years (1934–1948) with attention to American penal philosophy and practice.

Special thanks to Michael Spiegel and his shirt.

INDEX